AUTHOR

Roy Horton is the head instructor at Drone School UK.

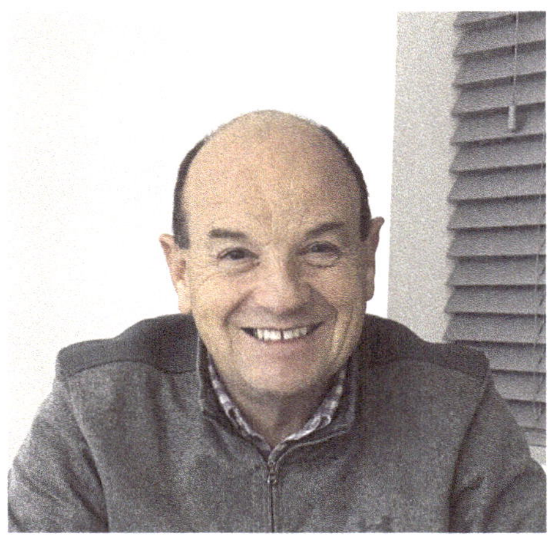

Roy has been teaching students to fly drones for over seven years on Face to Face courses at five locations throughout the UK. He has trained over 4,000 students to fly drones.

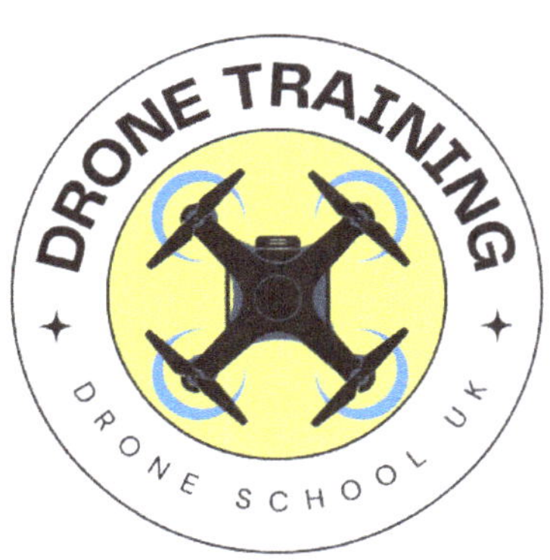

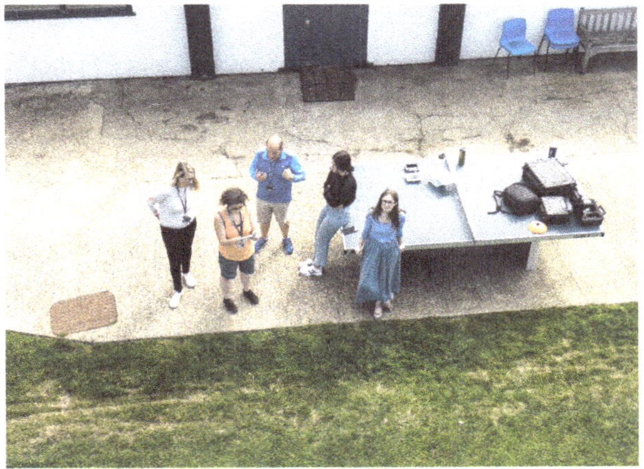

Roy also has a commercial drone business and has photographed many iconic scenes throughout the UK and South West from the air with his drones.

Table Of Contents

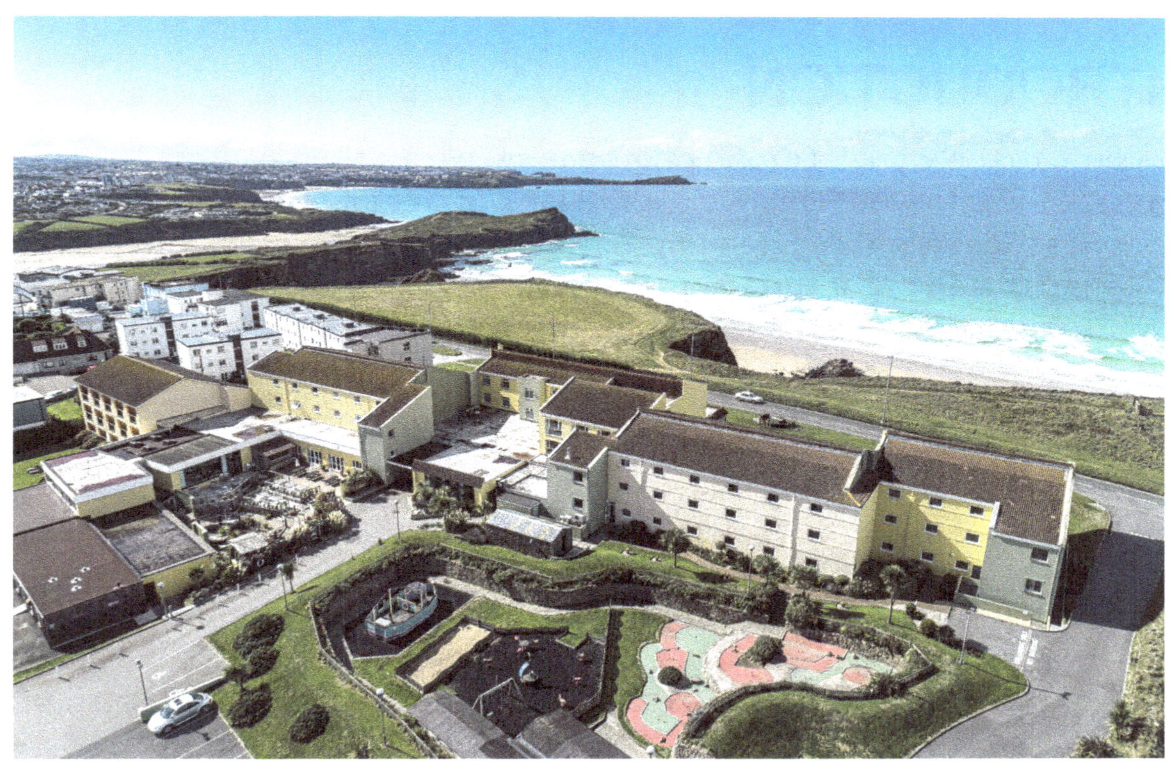

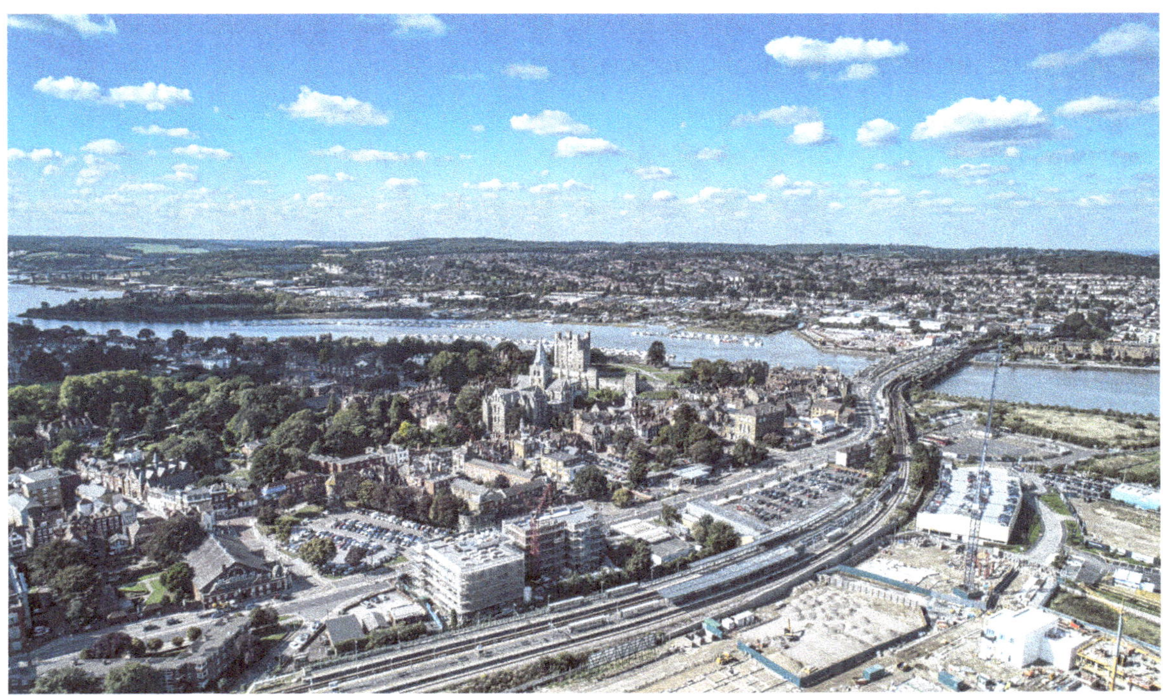

INTRODUCTION

Welcome to the world of drone photography, where the sky is not the limit but the canvas for your creative expressions. In this journey, we'll unravel the mysteries of aerial photography, from the basics of drone selection to mastering the art of capturing breathtaking images up to 400ft above the ground. This guide is your passport to the captivating world of aerial imagery.

The Aerial Perspective: Unleashing the Drone Vision

Drone Photography is more than just a hobby; it's a dynamic form of art that lets you freeze time from a celestial viewpoint. At it's core, drone photography is about breaking free from the constraints of traditional photography. It's about seeing the world from a new angle, literally and figuratively. The ability to elevate your perspective, opens up a world of exciting possibilities. Aerial photography with drones doesn't just capture images; it seizes emotions, stories, and unique angles that ground-level photography can only dream of.

In this guide, we'll focus on two exciting genres of aerial photography: property and landscape aerial photography.

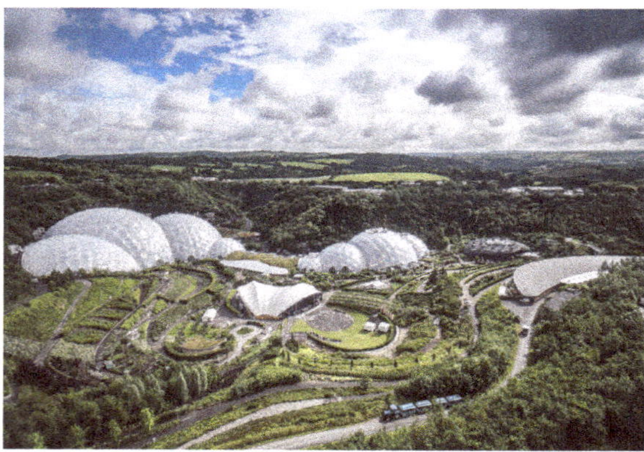
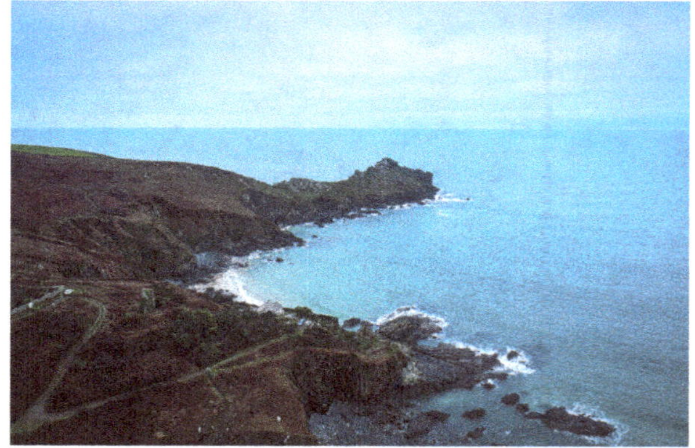

These genres offer a perfect starting point for beginners, presenting diverse subjects and techniques to explore. Imagine capturing the essence of a type of property or the majesty of a natural landscape, all seen on the ground in your drone's controller.

Choosing a Drone

Before you embark on your airborne adventures, let's introduce you to the drones. The market leader for consumer and business drones is the Chinese company - DJI. They come in various shapes and sizes, each equipped with cameras, catering to different skill levels and preferences. From compact (mini) drones suitable for beginners to advanced models with cutting-edge technology, your choice of drone will shape your aer al journey.

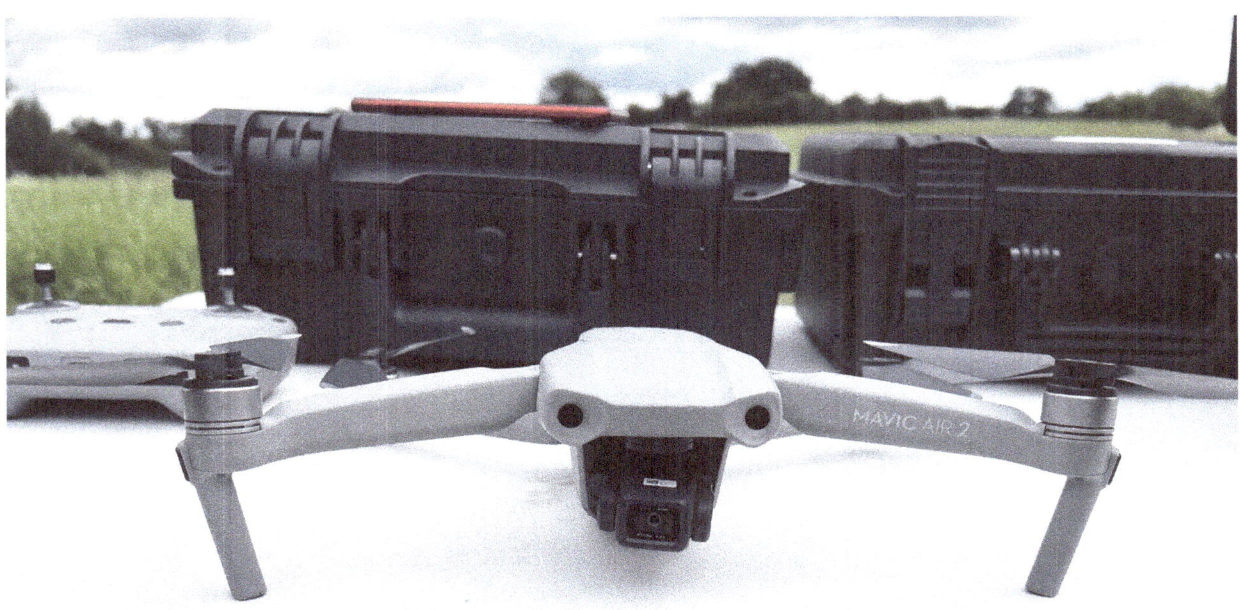

Consider factors such as flight time, camera quality, weight under or over 250 grams and ease of use when selecting your drone. Beginners might find joy in user-friendly models that prioritize stability and simplicity, while enthusiasts may opt for more advanced drones with manual controls and high-resolution cameras.

Research and choose a drone that aligns with your budget, skill level and aspirations, for a smooth takeoff for your aerial visions. Here are the current selection of DJI drones available in December 2023.

Which Drone Is Right for Me?

Aerial Photography   Immersive Flight   Aerial Cinematic Tools

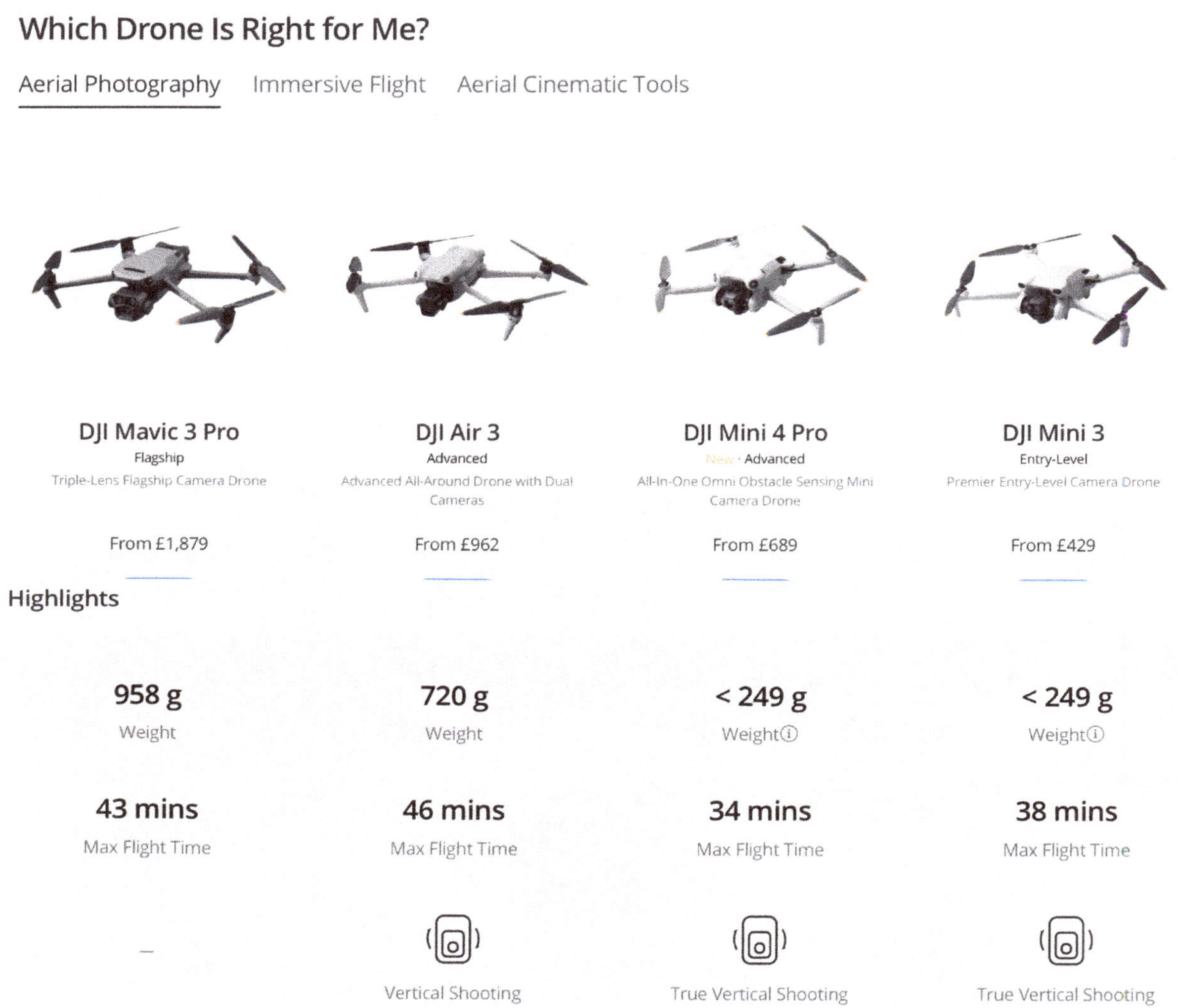

Highlights

Master the Basics

When you've chosen your drone, it's time to get acquainted with its eyes – the camera. From lenses to sensors, each component plays a crucial role in capturing the best images.

Lenses, the eyes of your drone, come in various shapes and sizes, each offering a unique perspective. Wide-angle lenses encompass sweeping landscapes, while telephoto lenses bring distant subjects up close.

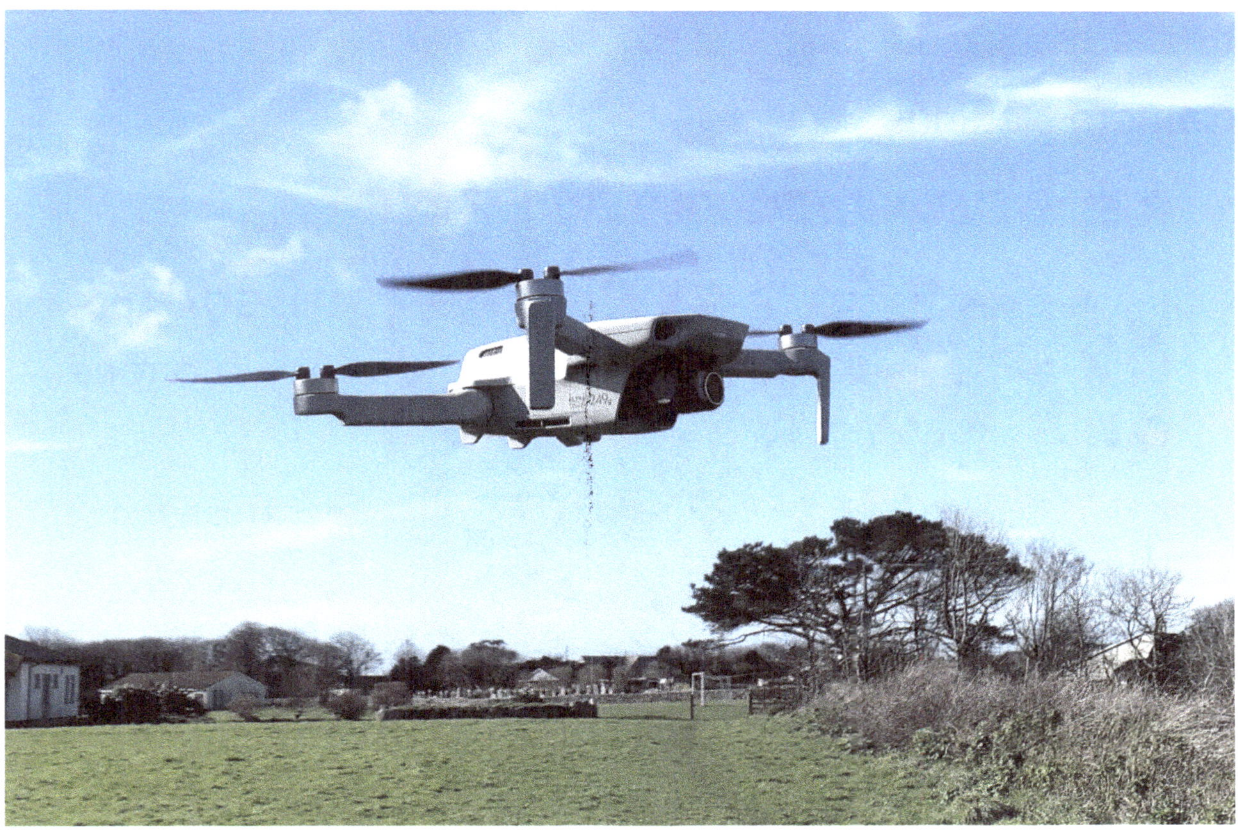

Beneath the lens lies the sensor, that captures light and transforms it in your photographs. Sensors come in various sizes, impacting image quality and performance. Larger sensors capture more light, perfect for detailed shots in low-light conditions. Smaller sensors, while capturing less light, still deliver impressive results in well-lit environments.

The buttons, dials, and menu options on your DJI drone's software app are the controls that empower you to shape your aerial narrative. Familiarise yourself with exposure settings, focus controls, and shooting modes. These controls grant you the power to adjust settings.

Learn the language of camera anatomy, and you can begin to turn your creative vision into stunning aerial images. We'll guide you through these concepts with the experience of a seasoned aerial photographer, using an approach that ensures you not only understand but enjoy the learning process too.

Camera Settings

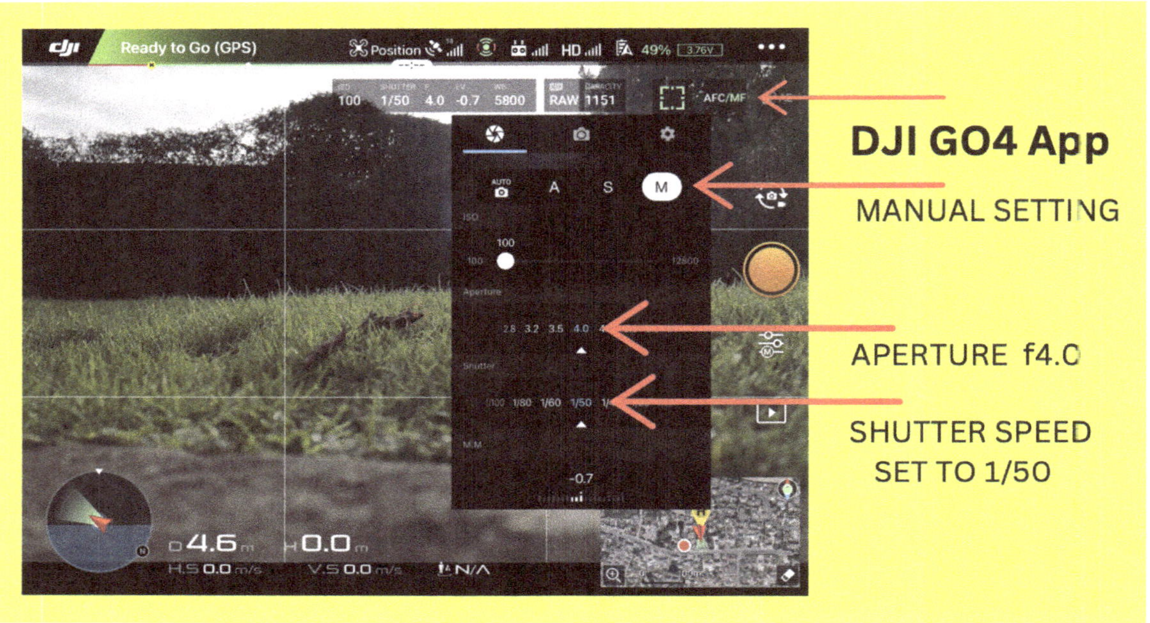

Let's look at camera settings. These settings include exposure, aperture, shutter speed, and ISO. Mastering the exposure triangle empowers you to control the balance of light in your images, using the interplay of aperture, shutter speed, and ISO, creating well-exposed aerial photographs.

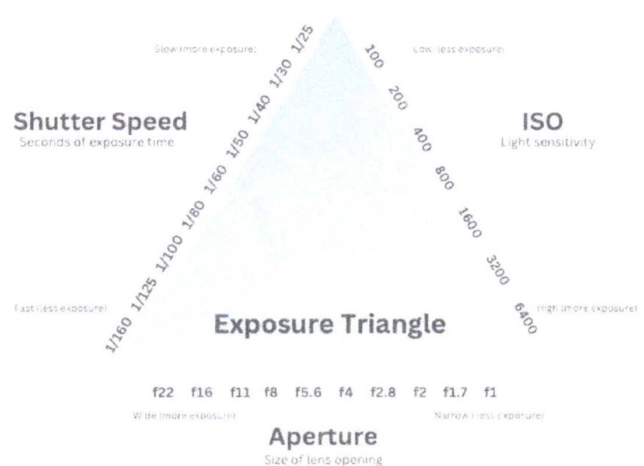

Balancing this trio ensures your aerial photographs are visually stunning, capturing the essence of the moment. Aperture, the eye of your lens, controls the depth of field, determining what's in focus. Shutter speed, the heartbeat of your camera, freezes or blurs motion, adding drama to your shots. ISO, the amplifier, boosts the sensitivity to light, allowing you to shoot in various lighting conditions.

Focus settings, dictate the sharpness and depth of your aerial compositions. Auto-focus is reliable for quick shots, while manual focus grants you the precision to capture intricate details. Explore the various focus modes, and you'll command the narrative focus of your aerial storytelling.

Shooting modes, offer a range of creative possibilities. Auto mode simplifies the process for beginners, while manual mode grants seasoned photographers' complete control. Depending on the complexity of the drone camera aperture and shutter priority modes strike a balance between automation and manual control, providing flexibility in different shooting scenarios.

The Essentials of Aerial Composition and Focus

Understanding composition is the final stroke for your aerial images. Rule of thirds, leading lines, and framing techniques become your allies as you frame each aerial shot with intention and creativity. Think of it as the art of arranging elements in the sky to tell a compelling visual story. Consider the placement of subjects in the frame, perspective, balance, symmetry of elements, and the natural flow of the scene.

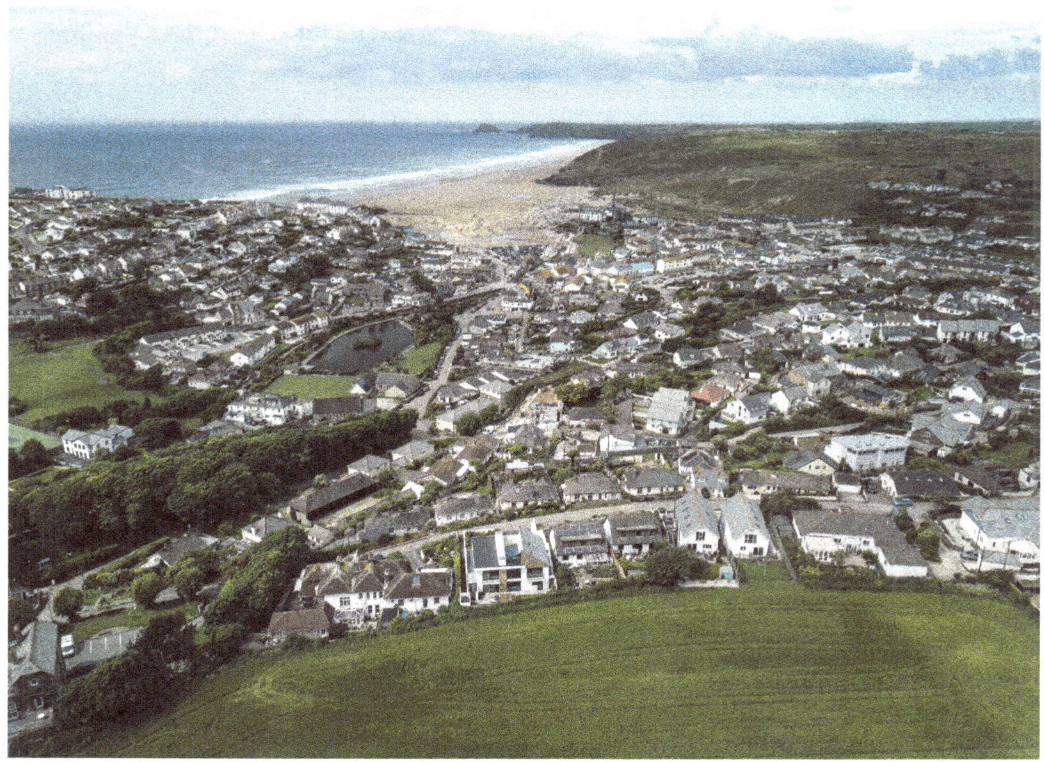

Experiment with different angles and perspectives, taking advantage of your drone's ability to explore unconventional vantage points. Embrace the vastness of the sky as your backdrop, and let your creativity soar as you compose visually striking aerial images.

Mastering focus allows you to control the narrative of your aerial story. Focus on focus! Experiment with different focus modes to sharpen your aerial storytelling skills. Composition, the arrangement of elements in your frame, is your artistic signature.

Practical Tips for Stunning Aerial Shots

Here are some practical tips to ensure your aerial adventure is smooth and your photographs are nothing short of spectacular:

1. Scout Your Location: Before take-off, scout the area for potential hazards and interesting subjects. Plan your flight path to capture the most compelling shots.

2. Check the Weather: The skies can be moody, so keep an eye on the weather conditions. Ideal lighting enhances your photographs, and clear skies provide the best visibility for navigation.

3. Understand Local Regulations: Familiarise yourself with local drone regulations and airspace restrictions. Ensuring you comply with rules keeps both your drone and the skies safe.

4. Practice Safe Flying: Start with open spaces away from obstacles, people, and wildlife. Practice basic manoeuvres to build confidence before attempting complex shots.

5. Master Your Drone's Flight Modes: Different drones offer various flight modes. Whether it's GPS-assisted hovering or follow modes, understand how to use these features to your advantage for smoother flights and more dynamic shots.

6. Experiment with Angles and Perspectives: The beauty of drone photography lies in its ability to explore new angles. Experiment with high and low perspectives, tilting the camera for dramatic shots, and discovering unique vantage points.

7. Capture Golden Hours: Sunrise and sunset provide magical lighting conditions known as the golden hours. Take advantage of these periods for warm, soft, and cinematic aerial shots.

8. Edit with Precision: Post-processing is the final touch to your aerial masterpieces. Use photo editing software to fine-tune exposure, colour balance, and sharpness for that polished finish.

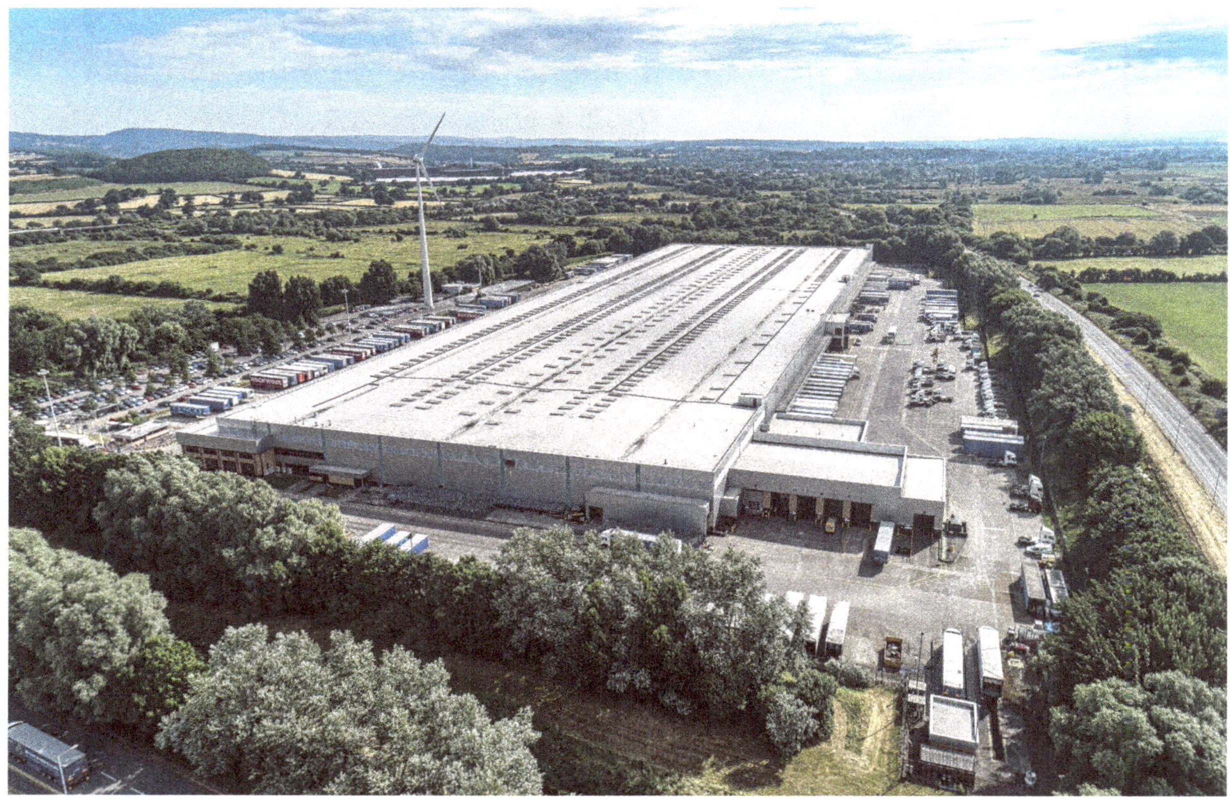

You've now embarked on a journey through the fascinating world of drone photography. From selecting your drone to mastering the nuances of camera and settings, you're well-equipped to capture breathtaking images from the skies.

Drone Rules and Regulations

The UK drone rules and regulations are outlined in this 15 minute video below: Learn all the important 2023 UK drone laws in 15 mins - 80% Knowledge in 20% of the time.

The US FAA rules are different fro the UK. there are two Youtube videos on my channel covering the rules in detail: FAA Drone Rules - PART 1- 10 key Questions ANSWERED before you fly any drone in the U.S.

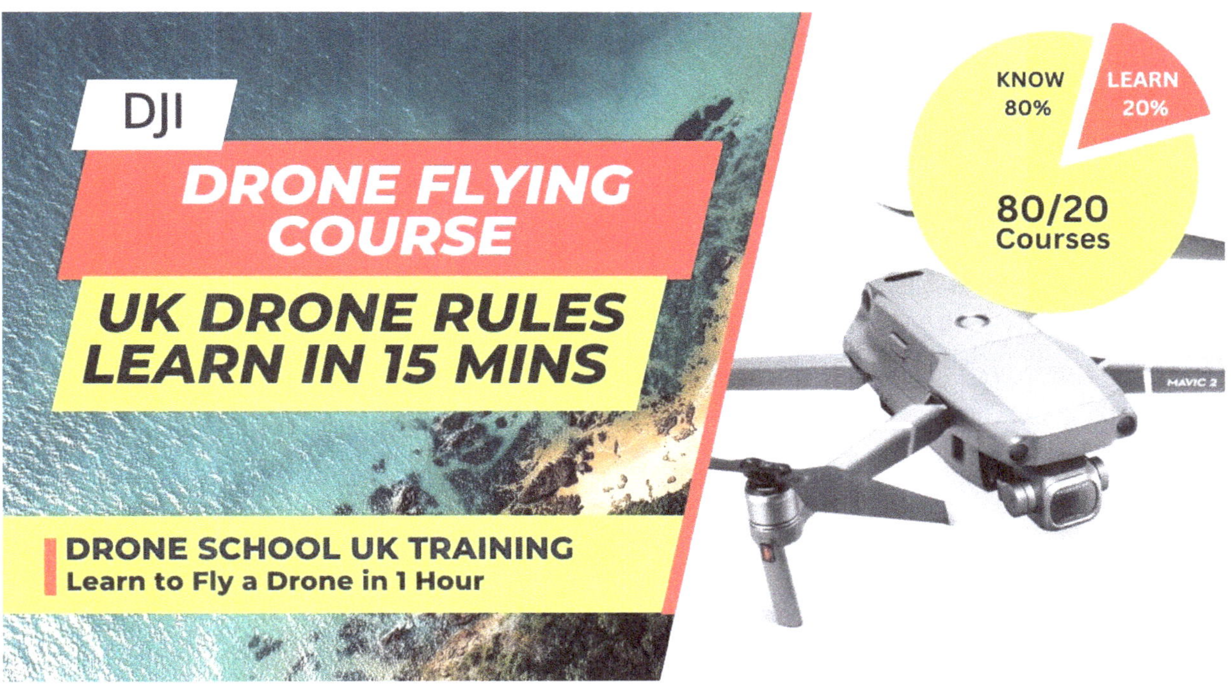

Revisit these pages, let the knowledge sink in, and don't hesitate to take your drone on numerous flights. Experiment with different genres, lenses, and settings – for your drone is not just a tool; it's an extension of your creative soul. The skies are your playground, and each flight is an opportunity to capture moments, tell stories, and create aerial masterpieces that reflect your unique vision.

Happy drone flying !!

DRONE CAMERAS

Drone Camera Anatomy

As you embark on this high-flying adventure with your drone camera, understanding its anatomy is the key to unleashing your creative potential. In this section, we'll look at the essential components of your drone's camera system, from the lenses that act as its eyes to the controls that give you the power to capture breathtaking shots.

1. Lenses: The Eye of the Drone

Imagine the lenses of your drone camera as the eyes that witness the world from above. These lenses come in various shapes and sizes, each offering a unique perspective on the landscape below. Selecting the appropriate lens for your drone can significantly impact the composition and look of your images.

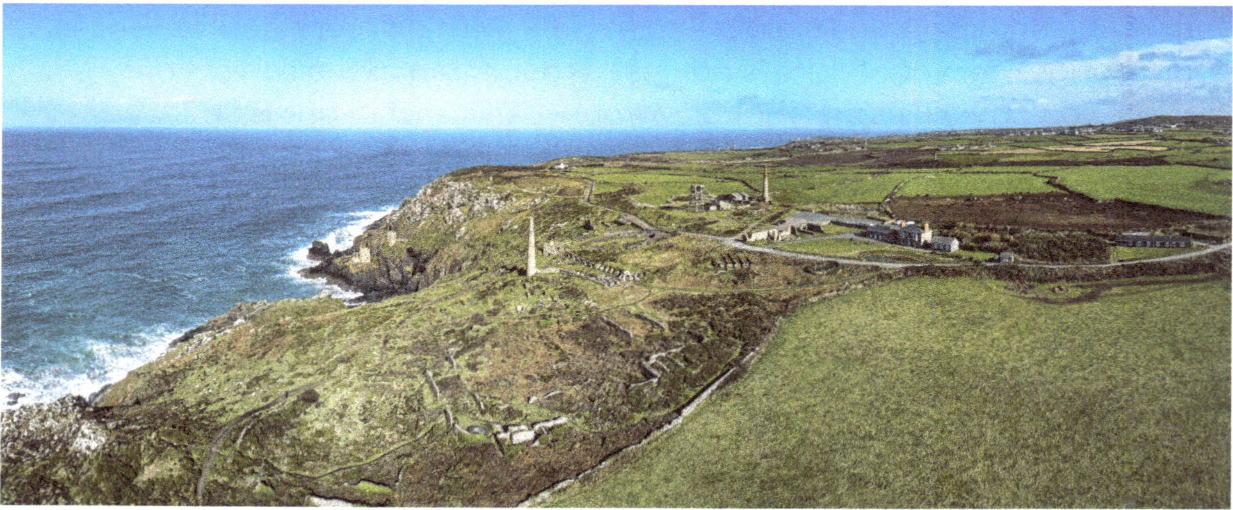

There are wide-angle lenses that capture expansive vistas, perfect for sweeping landscapes or cityscapes. Telephoto lenses, on the other hard, let you bring distant subjects up close, making them ideal for detailed shots of architecture from 50-150m away from the subject.

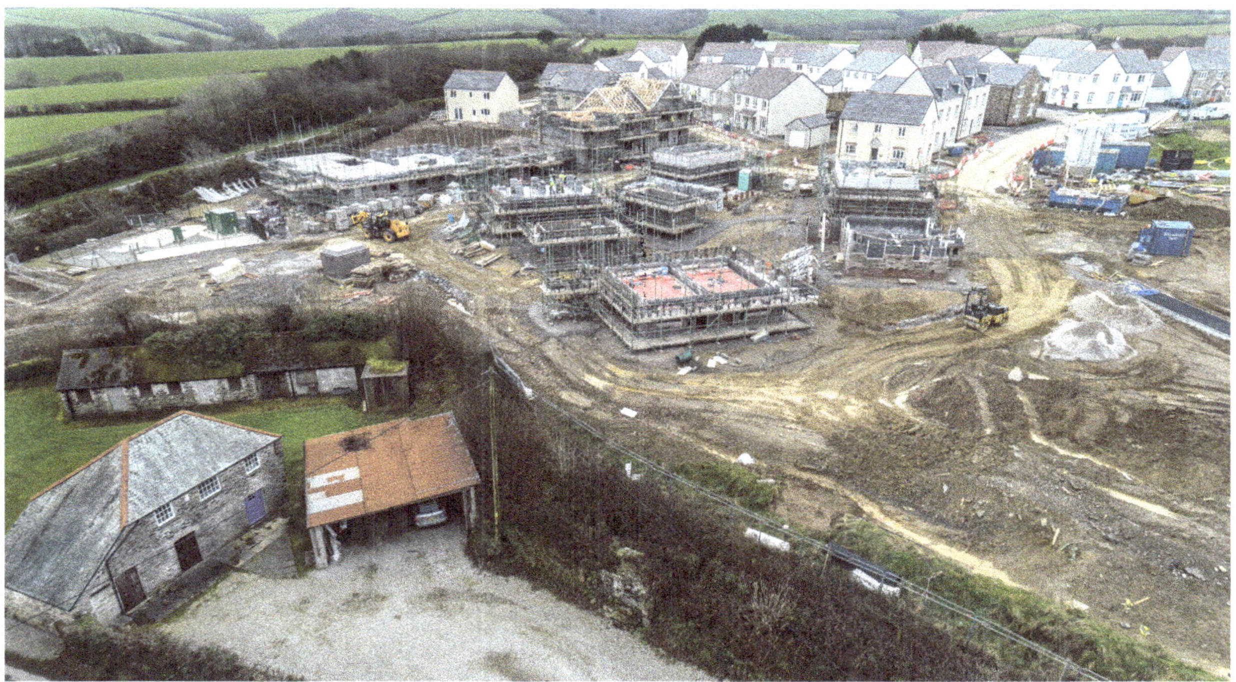

Understanding the characteristics of different lenses lets you choose the right one for the job, giving your aerial photographs that professional edge. So, don't be shy – experiment with various lenses.

2. Sensors: The Illuminator

Behind your drone's lens lies the camera sensor. This piece of technology transforms beams of light into the pixels that compose your aerial images. Larger more expensive sensors generally excel in capturing more light, resulting in sharper and more detailed images. They perform better in low-light conditions, allowing you to extend your photography into the twilight hours ensuring your dusk and dawn escapades are in vivid detail. On the other hand, smaller sensors on mini drones might not capture as much light but can still deliver impressive results in well-lit environments.

Embrace its capabilities, experiment with different lighting conditions, and watch as your aerial images unfold with every click of the shutter.

Here is the DJI Mavic 3 Pro with three Lenses in one gimbal

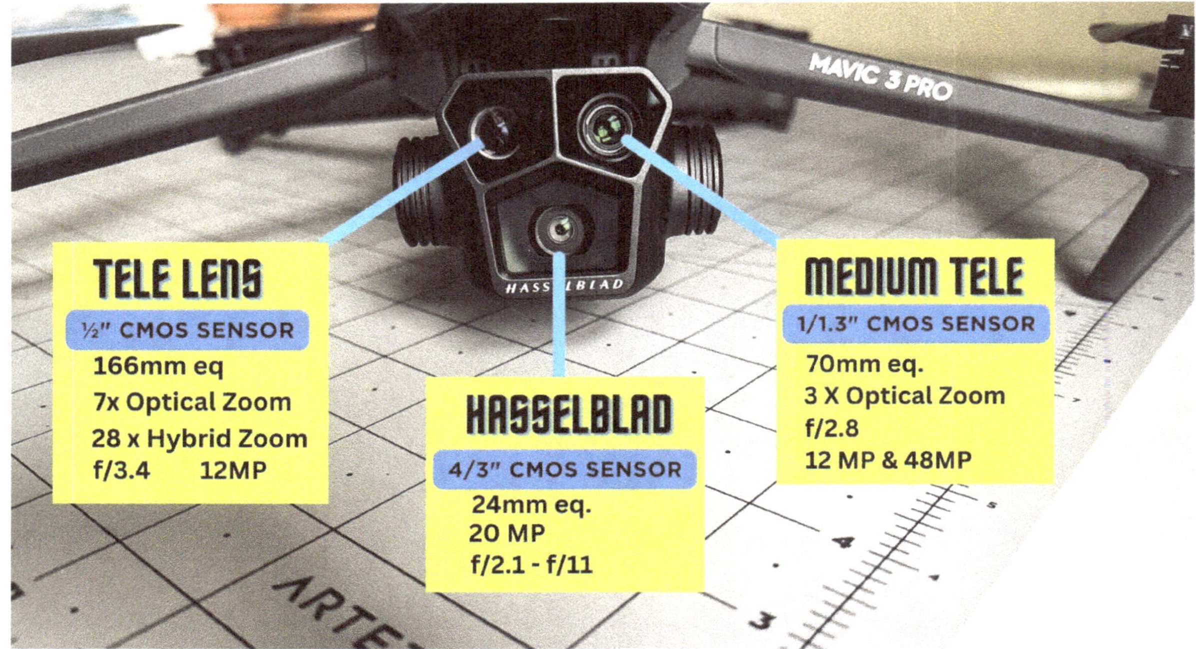

3. Controls: Navigation

Now, let's navigate the buttons, and menu options of your drone's software app. Think of these controls as learning the language of your drone camera - exposure, focus, and shooting modes. These controls give you the power to tailor your settings, ensuring each photograph reflects your creative vision.

Consider the exposure control, as your passport to mastering the balance of light in your images. Adjusting settings such as aperture, shutter speed, and ISO allows you to create well-exposed photographs, even in challenging lighting conditions.

Experiment with focus controls using Auto-focus for quick and convenient shots, while manual focus provides the precision needed for capturing intricate details. Your drone's ability to adapt to different focus modes is your ticket to achieving sharp, well-defined images in any scenario.

Shooting modes, offer a spectrum of creative possibilities. Auto mode simplifies the process for beginners, while manual mode grants full control to the seasoned photographers seeking the ultimate creative freedom. Aperture and shutter priority modes (semi-auto) strike a balance between automation and manual control, catering to various shooting situations with ease.

Mastering these controls transforms your drone camera from mere average into a tool of artistic expression. So, take the time to navigate through the menu options, press those buttons, and dial in your settings. With every adjustment, you shape the story of your aerial adventure.

In the DJI GO 4 Ap and Fly App there are a selection of different types of photos you can take with your drone camera.

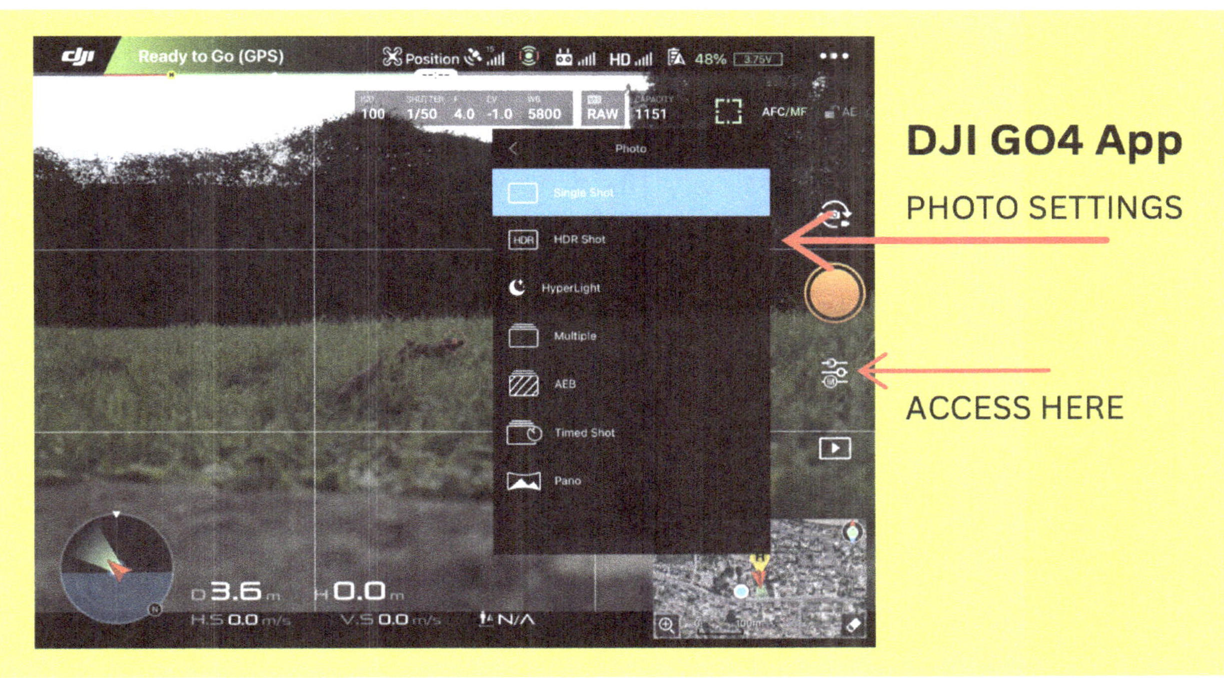

The photo menu above in the DJI GO 4 app shows the selection. Single, HDR shot and AEB are covered in detail later in this guide.

HyperLight - Is for low light conditions featured on the Mavic 2 Pro.

Multiple: The camera will take multiple pictures (3 or 5) when you press the shoot button. You might want to use this mode if you are trying to get a shot of a moving subject.

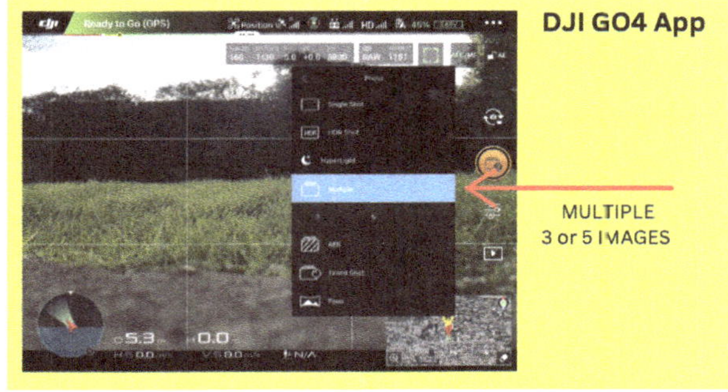

Timed: This takes timed shots that can be used to create time-lapses. You can choose a time interval. Depending on the drone the lowest interval is 2s. Minimum of 24/25 photos are needed to make a one second video.

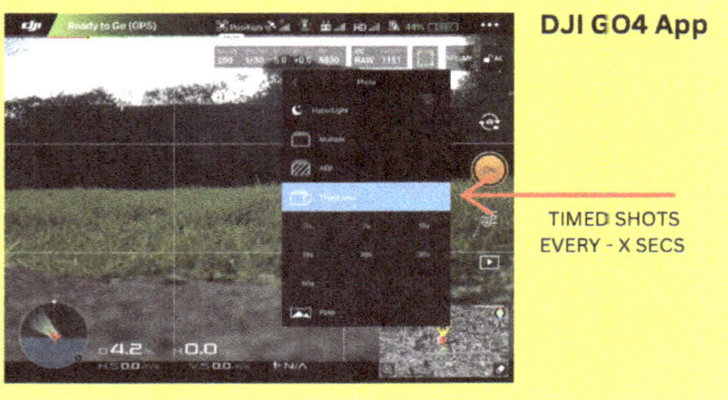

Pano: The camera takes a number of photos depending on the type of panorama selected and the DJI drone used. 180 and Vertical panos take 3 images and stitch them together. 360 panoramas take a minimum of 26 images and stitch them together. The images can be stitched by the DJI App or exported to other software like PTGUI for better results.

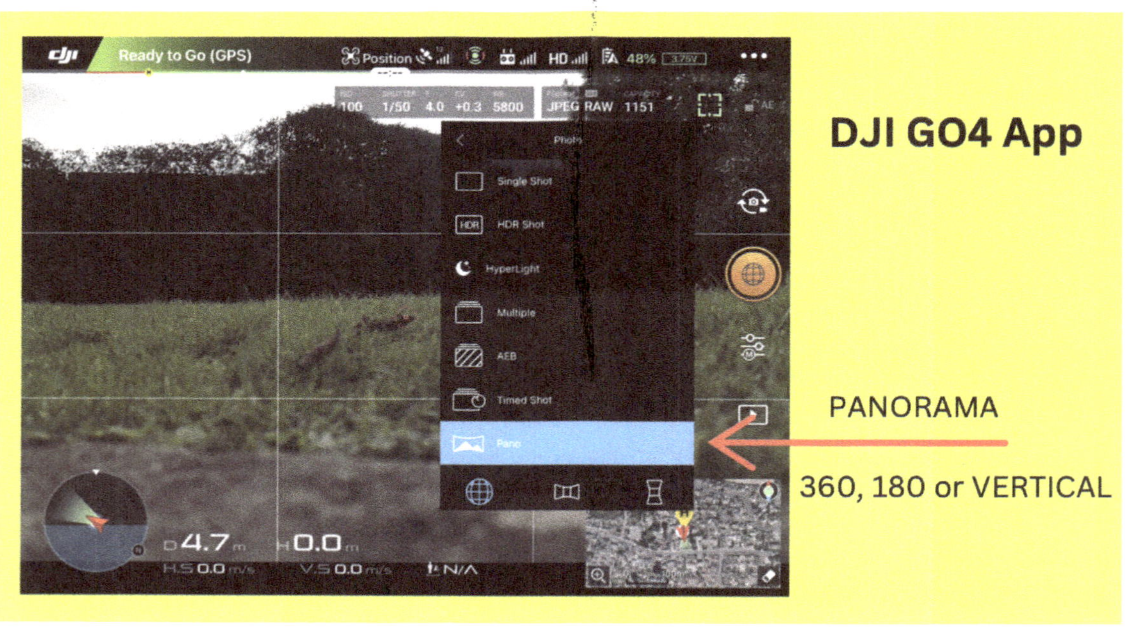

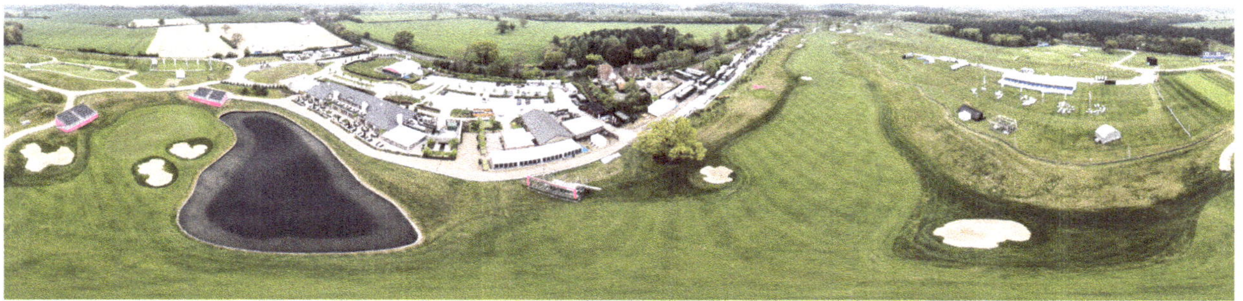

Essential Drone Camera Settings

Now that you've become acquainted with the components of your drone camera, let's look into the essential settings that will elevate your aerial photography.

1. Exposure Settings: The Illuminating Triangle

Welcome to the exposure triangle – the choreography of aperture, shutter speed, and ISO.

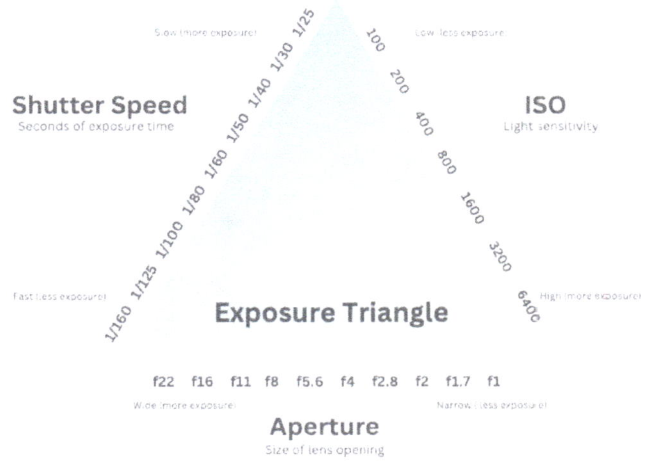

These three sides of the triangle are the basis of well-exposed images, and understanding their delicate dance is the key to unlocking the secrets of aerial photography.

Aperture controls the size of the lens opening, determining the amount of light that enters. Shutter speed dictates how long the dance lasts, capturing motion or freezing it in time. ISO amplifies the dancers' energy, compensating for low-light situations. Together, they craft well-exposed images that dance harmoniously between light and shadow.

Understanding this dance allows you to create well-exposed images tailored to your creative vision. Need to freeze the action of a bustling cityscape? Increase the shutter speed. Want a dreamy, blurred effect of a flowing river? Opt for a slower shutter speed. The exposure triangle is your playbook for orchestrating the perfect aerial performance.

2. Focus Settings: Sharpening Your Skyline

In the skies, focus is paramount, it dictates where the audience's attention should lie. Explore the different focus modes at your disposal, starting with the reliable auto-focus that is quick, convenient, and perfect for capturing spontaneous moments or when you're in a time crunch.

On the other hand, manual focus is your opportunity to shape the narrative with precision. Use it to highlight specific details or create stunning depth in your aerial compositions.

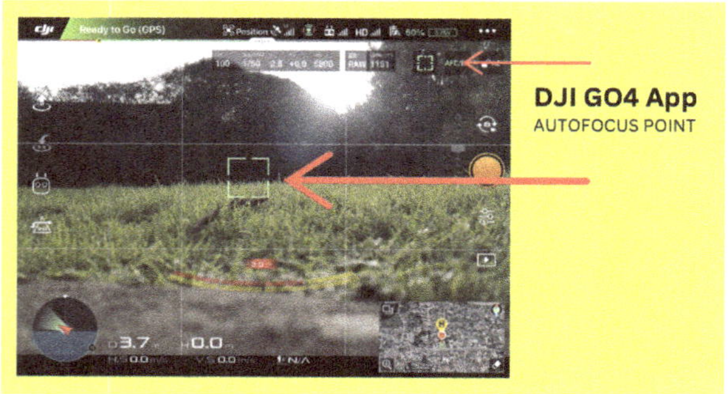

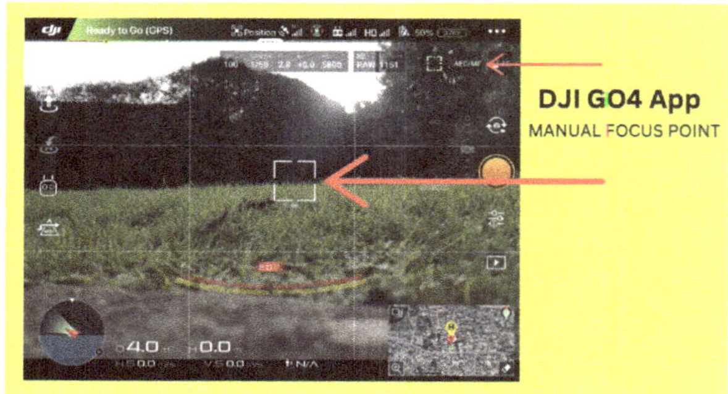

Mastering focus settings ensures your aerial images are sharp and defined with a clear focus point.

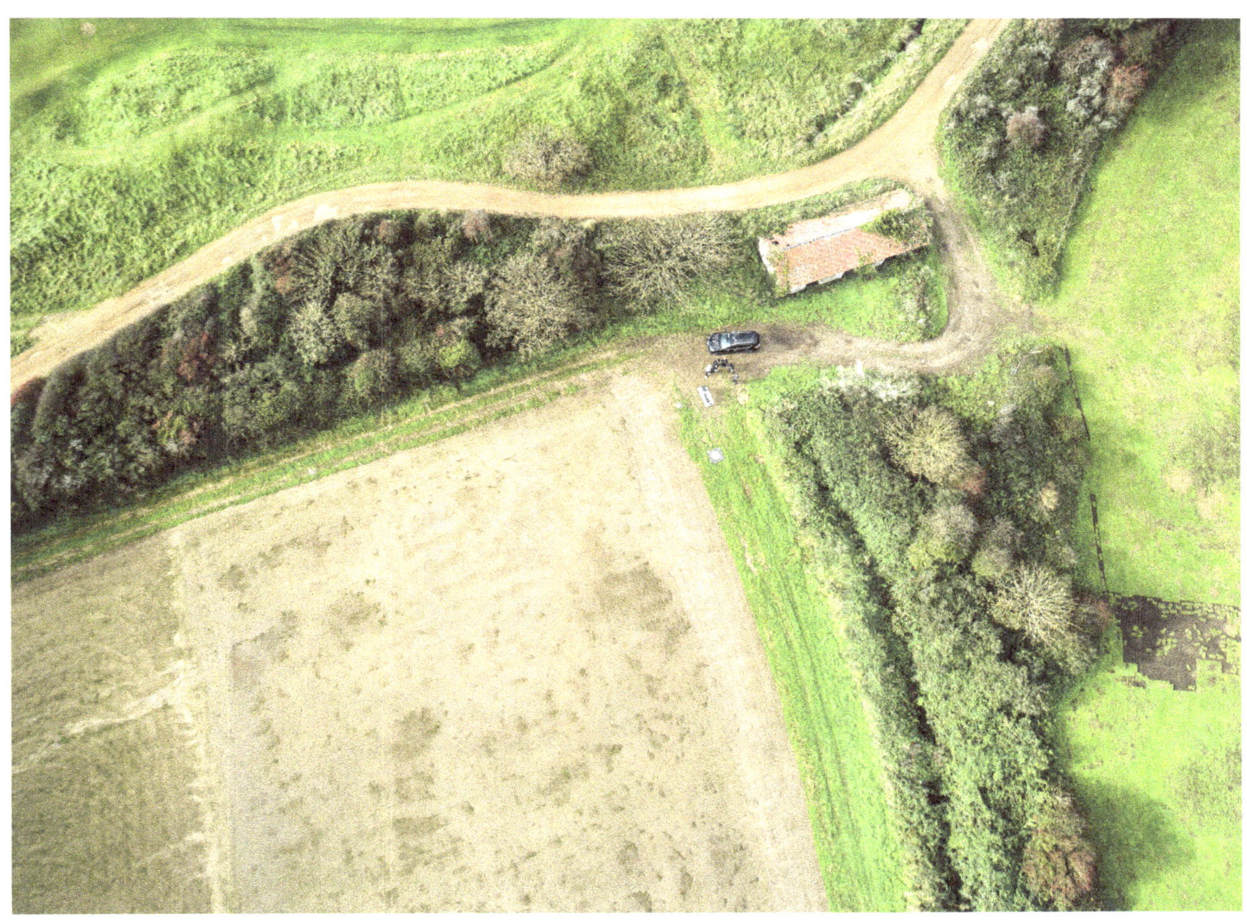

3. Shooting Modes: Crafting the Aerial Story

Your drone camera's shooting modes are the chapters in the book of your aerial adventure. Auto mode is the beginner's guide, handling most settings automatically for a hassle-free experience. As you gain confidence, venture into manual mode, where you have complete control over every aspect of your aerial narrative.

Aperture priority and shutter priority modes (Semi -Auto) are like choosing between different genres of storytelling. Aperture priority empowers you to control the depth of field, adding a cinematic touch to your aerial scenes. Shutter priority, on the other hand, lets you capture motion in the sky, freezing or blurring elements to evoke emotion in your photographs.

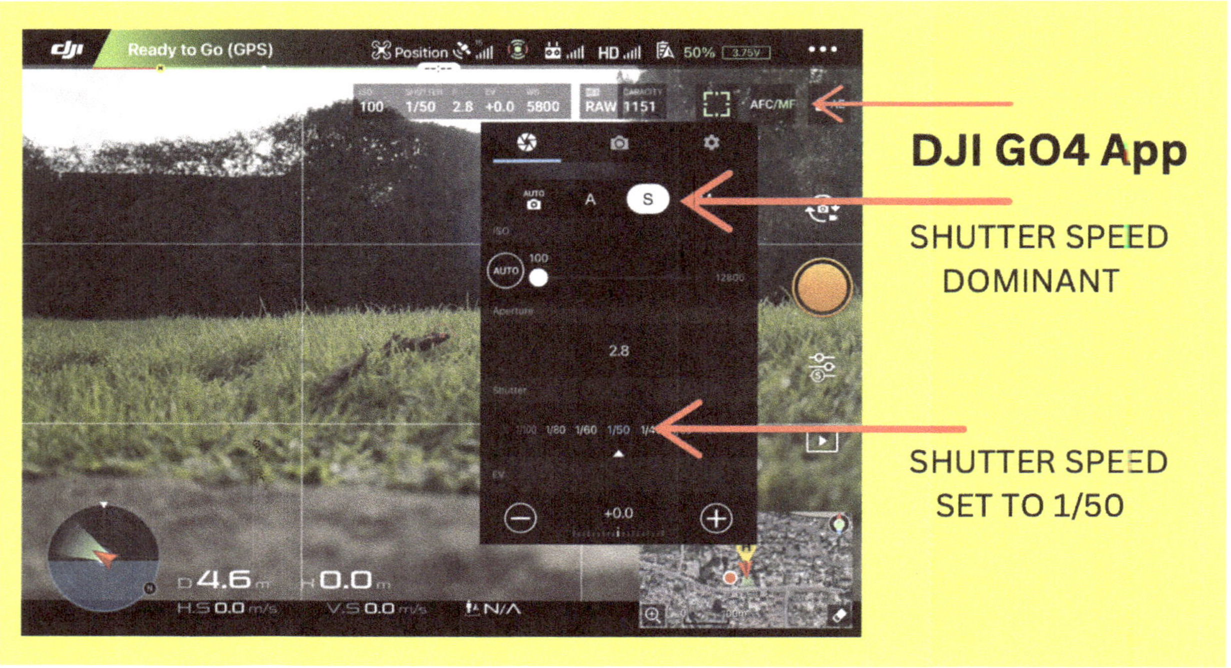

As you navigate through these semi auto shooting modes, think of them first as a manual setting with the others choosing an auto setting after.

The shutter speed sweet spot for most DJI Drones is 1/50. if shutter speed is priority (dominant), then the aperture and ISO will fall in behind the selected shutter speed.

The aperture sweet spot for most DJI Drones is f4.0 or f5.6, if aperture is priority (dominant), then the shutter speed and ISO will fall in behind the selected aperture.

 Experiment with each, discover your preferred style, and watch as your drone photography skills evolve into a captivating narrative.

FOCUS

Welcome to the fascinating world of camera focus, where the tiniest adjustments can transform your aerial snapshots from blurry mishaps to sharp still images. In this section, we'll embark on a journey through the art of focusing with your drone camera—a skill that is crucial. Let's go through auto-focus, manual focus, to achieve razor-sharp images with finesse and flair.

Auto-Focus and Manual Focus: The Dynamic Duo

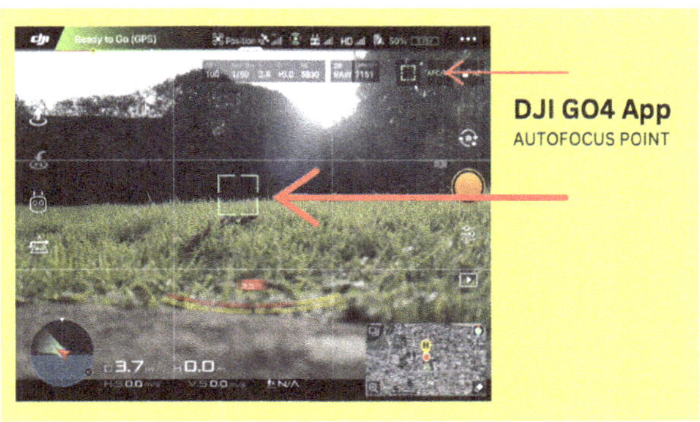

1. Auto-Focus: (AF): Most drone cameras come equipped with auto-focus systems that make your life a lot easier. Cn the drone controller there is an AF setting with a **GREEN** square as the aiming point for the auto focus.

2. Manual Focus: Now, let's take the reins into your hands literally. Manual focus is your secret weapon, it gives you absolute control over what's in focus. It gives you pinpoint targeting so hit MF on the drone and use the WHITE square to manually choose the focus point.

Practical Tip: *Manual focus shines in situations where your drone might get confused, like when shooting past branches or buildings.*

Sharpening Your Focus Techniques

Your drone camera is not a mind reader (yet), so you need to tell it where to focus. Being specific on your focus point makes all the difference to your image. Achieving sharp focus is the holy grail of drone photography, because you cannot use blurred images.

1. Focus Point Selection: Your drone camera allows you to choose where it locks onto focus within the frame. You can focus in the centre of the image or anywhere on the image. Try to use the four cross points in the rule of thirds lines for the best off-centre focussing results, steering the attention where it matters most.

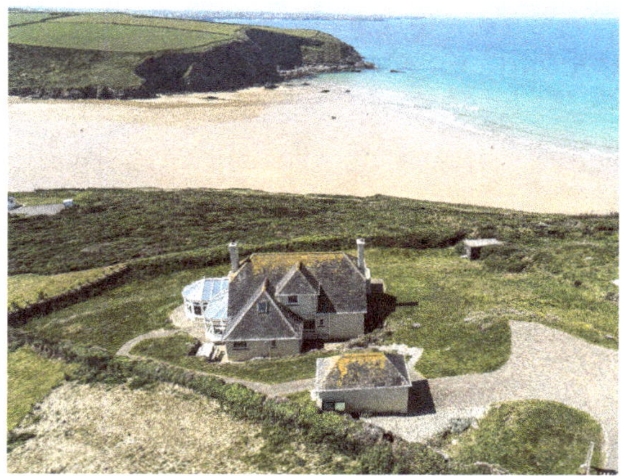

Practical Tip: *When shooting a stunning landscape, place your focus point on the prominent feature, like a lone building.*

Practical Tip: *Take a number of photos of the same scene by experimenting with different focus points to add depth and interest to your compositions.*

2. Depth of Field (DoF): The force that determines what's sharp and what's dreamy in your photo. Different apertures influence the depth of field and this opens up a realm of creative possibilities. Smaller and cheaper drones may just have fixed aperture cameras, so the DoF can only be achieved with key focus points.

Practical Tip: *Smaller apertures (higher f-numbers) create a deeper DoF, ideal for capturing vast landscapes in crystal-clear detail.*

Practical Tip: *Use a wide aperture (low f-number) for striking foreground objects in focus with a blurred background.*

3. Focusing in Low Light: At twilight, Nightfall or stormy skies focusing in low-light conditions can feel like searching for your keys in the dark. The low-light focusing challenges can be helped by increasing the ISO (too much ISO can cause digital noise in the image - graininess) or slowing the shutter speed to allow more light into the image.

Practical Tip: *In low-light situations, switch your drone camera to manual focus for more control.*

Practical Tip: *Increase your ISO settings in low light to assist your camera in achieving focus.*

In conclusion, embrace focus, experiment with its varied forms, and let your creativity soar with every click of the shutter. Experiment with Auto and Manual focus and lots of focus points in your images. Do this while the drone is in the air, take a wide selection of images, so you are not thinking of what might have been, when you get back and are viewing and editing your photos.

COMPOSITION

Welcome, to composition – the secret sauce that transforms ordinary images into works of art. Understanding and knowing the principles of composition will help you to see why certain images of the same scene stand out and are so much better than the others. Here are practical techniques and wisdom to elevate your drone photographs to new heights!

Unlocking the Power of Composition

Composition is not just about putting things in your frame; it's about arranging them in a way that tells a compelling story. Think of your aerial photograph as a canvas, and composition as your brush strokes. Whether you're capturing the sprawl of a town or the majesty of a mountain range, understanding the principles of composition will transform your aerial images into captivating tales.

Let's navigate through concepts such as the rule of thirds, leading lines, framing, and the magic of perspective and depth. These are not just technical terms; they are your tools to create interest, guiding the viewer's eyes and infusing energy into your aerial images.

Improving Your Compositions: Rule of Thirds in Action

1. What is the Rule of Thirds? This principle involves dividing your frame into a 3x3 grid creating nine equal sections. Then strategically placing key elements along the gridlines or at their intersections. This seemingly simple act transforms your photographs, creating a dynamic and balanced visual experience.

Now, you might be thinking, "Why thirds? Why not quarters or halves?" Well, thirds strike the perfect balance – not too crowded, not too sparse. It's the Goldilocks zone of composition.

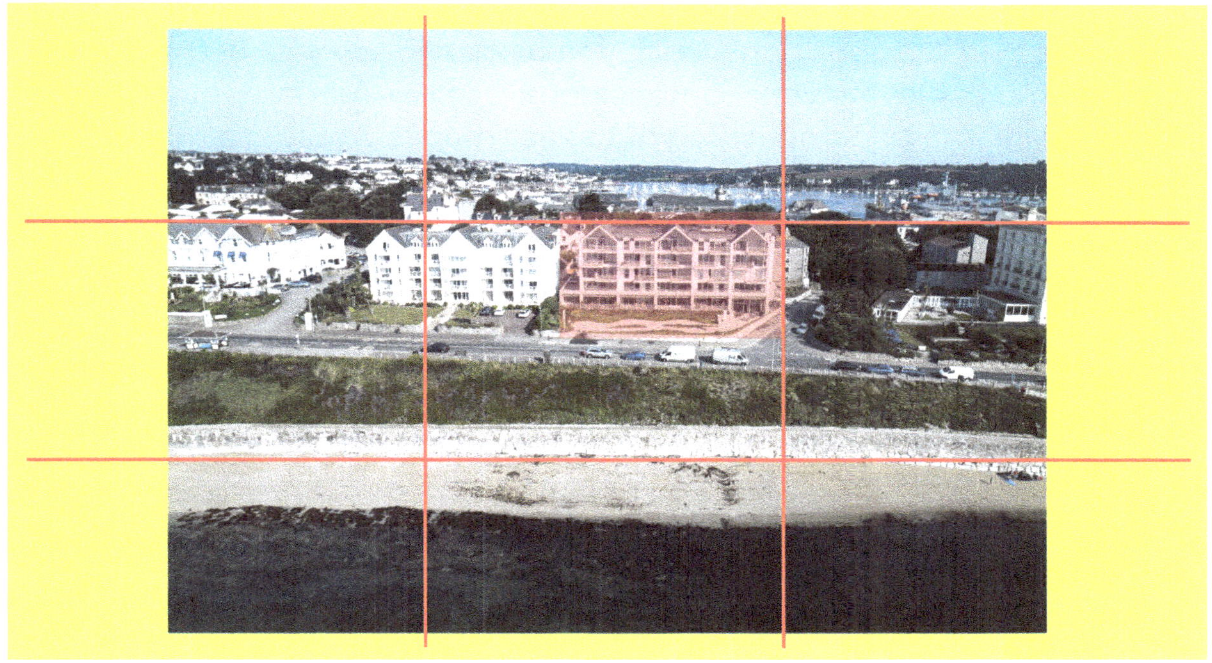

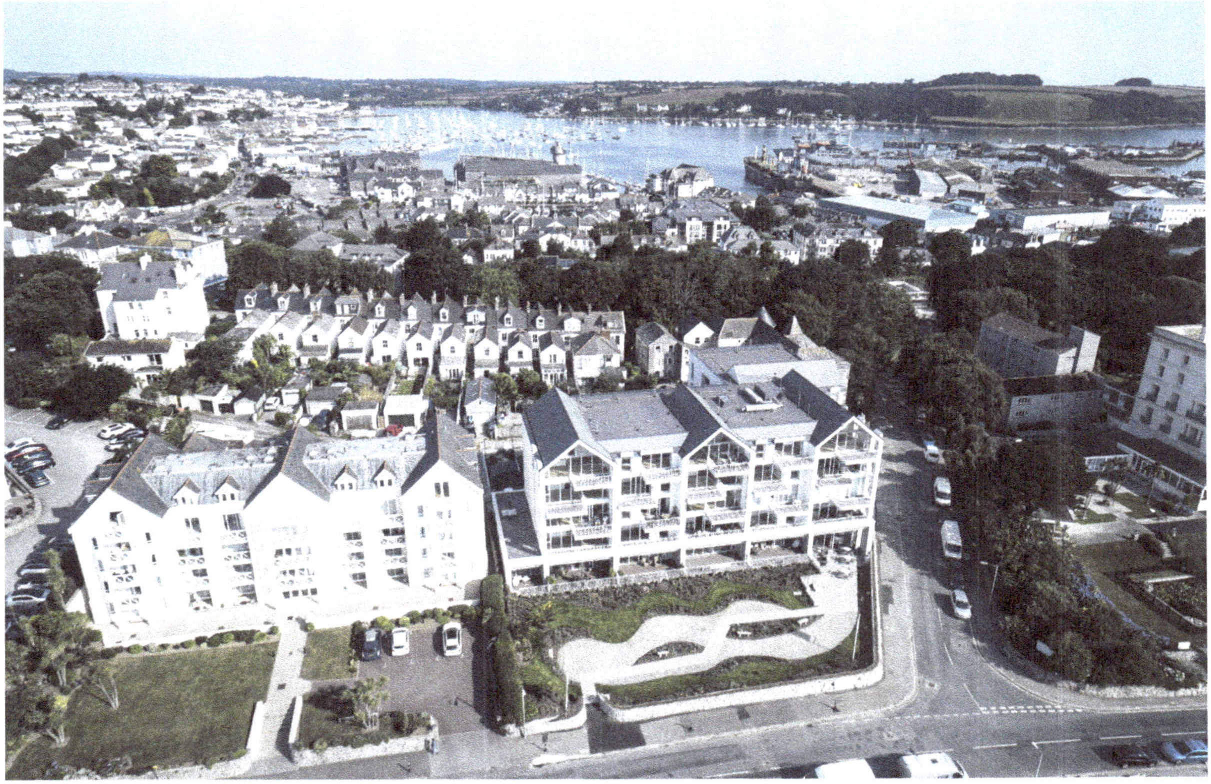

2. Improving Your Compositions: Once you grasp the essence of the Rule of Thirds, it's time to elevate your compositions. Use this fundamental rule to add interest, drama, and impact to your aerial images. Apply the rule in various scenarios, whether you're capturing vast landscapes, buildings, or objects.

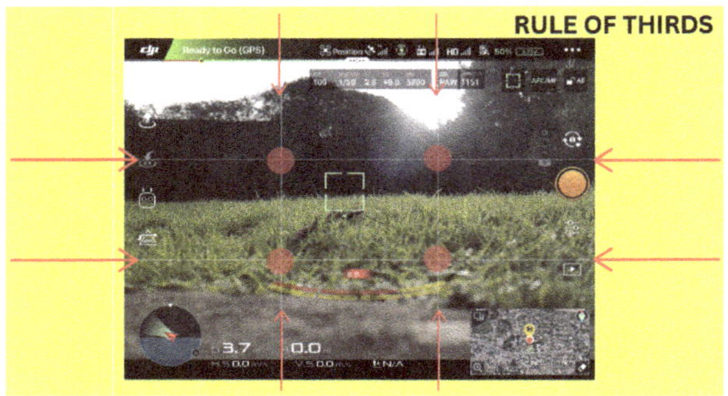

The drone controllers can have the Rule of Thirds enabled. When the drone is in the air change the pitch of the gimbal position on your main subject at the four different intersections and take a wide selection of images. You can always delete the poor ones later.

Remember, the Rule of Thirds is not a rigid law but a flexible guideline. Sometimes rules are made to be broken, but you need to understand them first.

Leading Lines and Framing

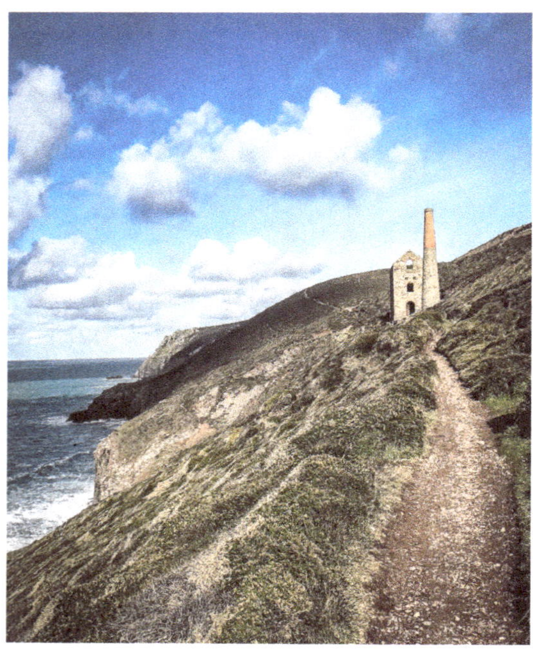

1. Leading lines: are like pathways, directing the viewer's gaze through your photograph. Whether it's a natural feature like a winding river, a man-made element like a road cutting through a field, shorelines or the curve of a mountain range, leading lines add a sense of direction and depth. Learn to identify and use these lines to create compelling compositions that draw your audience into the heart of your aerial story.

Understanding and utilising leading lines add a sense of depth and direction to your images.

When your drone is in the air you need to look for and identify them. From diagonals that add energy to horizontals that evoke tranquillity, you'll soon see the world as a canvas of lines waiting to be explored.

You can get an idea of views when you look around on the ground before your drone takes off, but things always look different when you view from 100, 200, and 400ft.

2. Framing: Imagine your frame as a window, and framing as the elegant drapes that draw attention to the view outside. That's where framing comes in. Framing involves using elements within your scene – be it tree branches, arches, or even clouds – to frame your subject, drawing attention to it like a spotlight on a stage. It's a powerful technique that adds emphasis and context, turning a simple subject into the focal point.

Perspective and Depth in Aerial Photography

Now, let's add a third dimension to your aerial photographs – perspective and depth. Imagine your photos not just as snapshots from the sky but as windows into a three-dimensional world. Understanding perspective is like seeing and making the aerial image in 3D.

1. Understanding Perspective: Perspective is the illusion of depth and distance in your images. It's influenced by choices such as focal length, shooting angle, and your distance from the subject. It's not just about where your drone hovers; it's about how you see the world from above. Practice is the best way to understand these elements.

Take several different images using the influence of focal length, shooting angle, and distance on perspective, ensuring you grasp the nuances of visual storytelling from the sky.

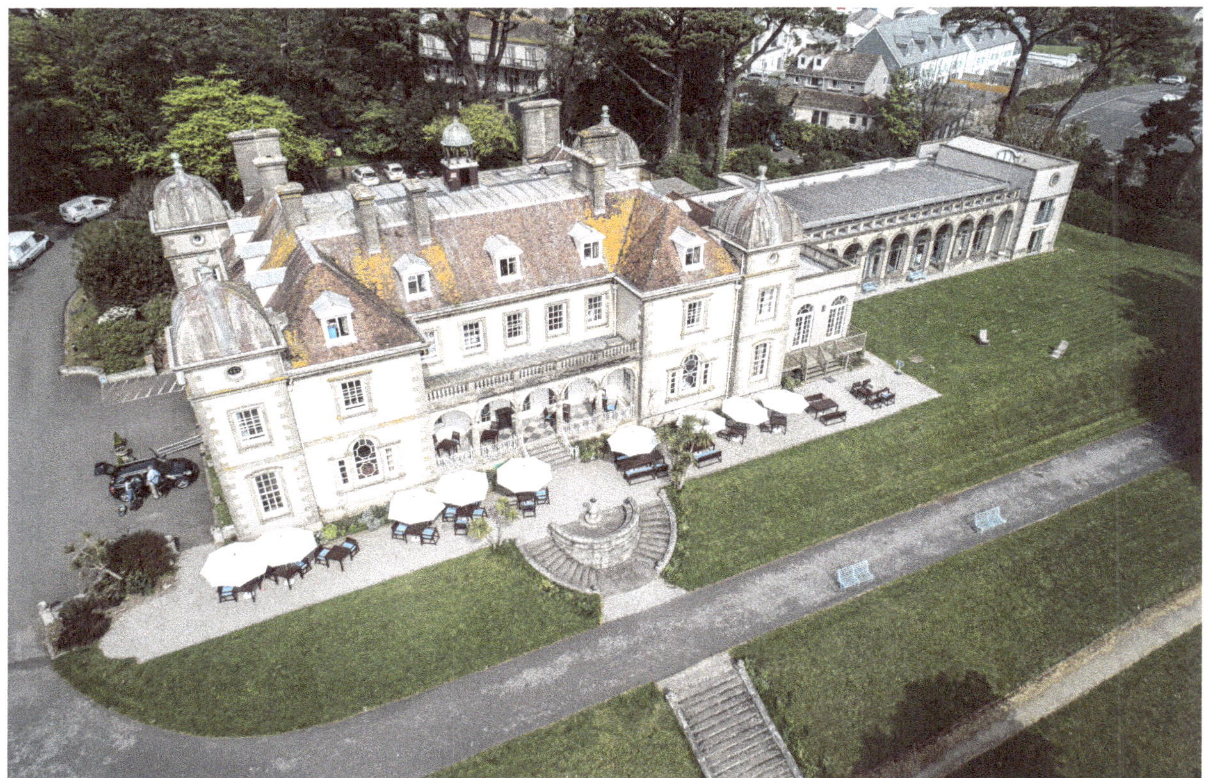

Perspective is the illusion of depth that pulls the viewer into your composition.

2. Creating Depth: Aerial photographs can sometimes feel flat, like a pancake in the sky. Start to include foreground elements, layering, and utilising perspective to create parallax, giving your photos that immersive, three-dimensional feel.

Forget about flat dull, two-dimensional photos; let's make your images pop with the depth and richness they deserve. With a bit of practice, you'll transform your aerial photographs from snapshots to visual adventures.

3. Overcoming Flatness: Picture this: a stunning aerial landscape that looks as flat as a pancake. We've all been there, and thought, "Something's missing". The culprit is often the lack of perspective and depth. Your aerial images must tell stories with layers, intrigue, and a sense of vastness that overcomes the flatness blues.

Look at the sky as a multidimensional canvas, where every element, from the foreground to the distant horizon, plays a role in crafting your aerial narratives. Learn to look beyond the flatness. Incorporate foreground elements, experiment with layering, and embrace the concept of perspective to add layers to your photographs.

1. Scout Your Location: Before taking flight, scout your location for interesting elements and potential compositions. Look for leading lines, natural features, structures, and unique perspectives that will add visual interest to your aerial photographs.

2. Experiment with Angles: The beauty of aerial photography is the freedom to explore various gimbal angles. Tilt your camera up or down, rotate your drone, and experiment with different perspectives to discover the most captivating compositions.

3. Fly to Different Altitudes: Adjusting your drone's altitude can significantly impact your composition. Higher altitudes may provide a broader perspective, while lower altitudes allow for more intimate and detailed shots. Experiment with different heights to find the sweet spot for each scenario. Take photos at all the altitudes you fly to.

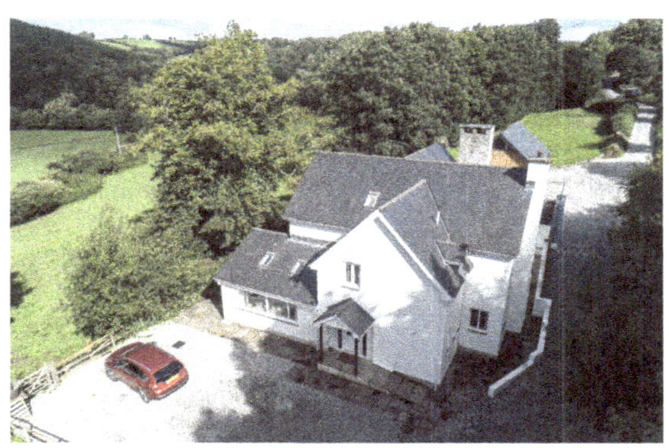
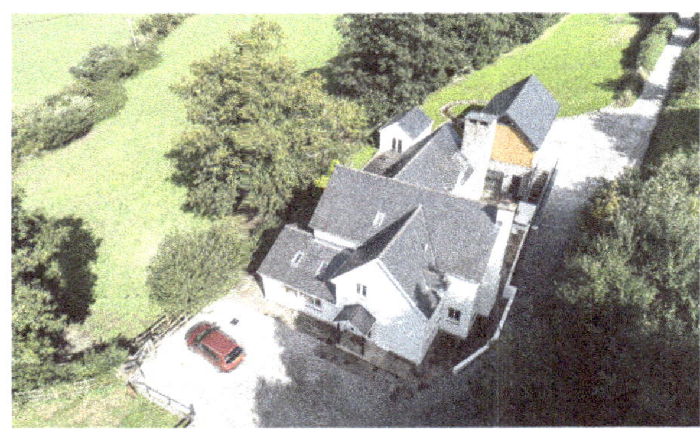

4. Timing is Everything: Consider the time of day and weather conditions when planning your aerial photography sessions. The golden hour, with its warm, soft light, can enhance the mood of your images, while clouds and dramatic skies add a touch of dynamism. Be patient and wait for the right moment to capture your aerial masterpiece.

5. Rule of Odds: The rule of odds suggests that an odd number of elements in your composition is more visually appealing than an even number. Consider this when framing your shots, especially when capturing groups of subjects or objects.

6. Experiment with Leading Lines: Leading lines can be found everywhere, from roads and rivers to the natural contours of the land. Experiment with using these lines to guide the viewer's eye through your composition and create a sense of movement.

7. Move the Horizon: While it's tempting to centre or put your horizon in the top third, don't be afraid to break the mould. Offsetting the horizon can add drama and interest to your aerial photographs. Experiment with unconventional horizon placements to see the impact on your composition. Take a wide selection of photos. It is easy and quick to move the gimbal up and down.

8. Balance Your Elements: Strive for balance in your compositions. If you have a dominant subject on one side, look for a major reflection element on the opposite side to create harmony and visual interest.

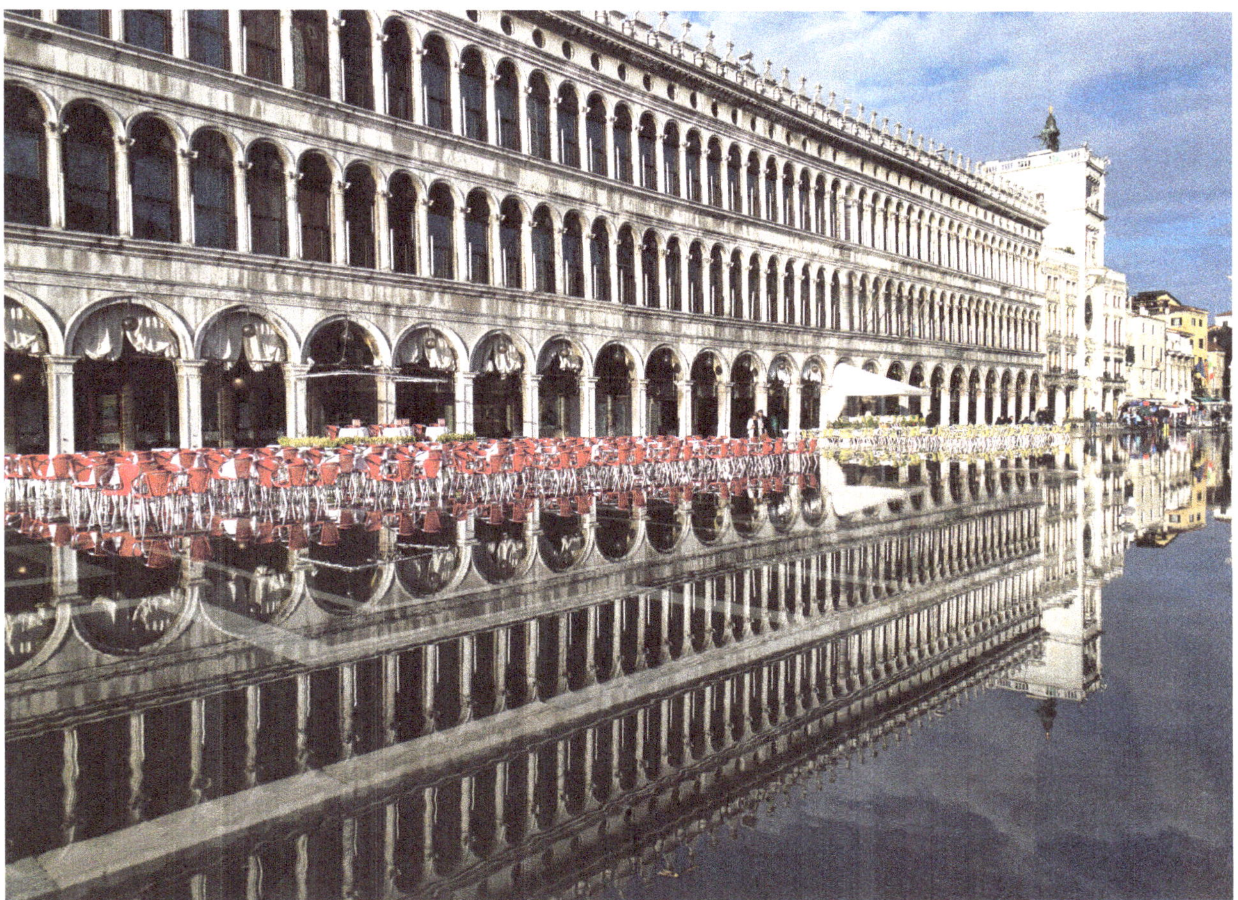

9. Post-Processing Magic: Don't shy away from post-processing tools to enhance your compositions. Adjusting contrast, saturation, and sharpening can bring out the details and fine-tune your aerial images for that extra wow factor.

Remember, there are no strict rules in composition – experiment and take the photo, you can always delete, and no one will ever judge it.

Make this knowledge your own. Revisit these concepts, practice with purpose, and let the principles of composition become second nature. As you navigate the skies with your drone, envision each frame as a canvas waiting for your artistic touch. Experiment with different compositions, play with perspectives, and let your creativity soar to new heights.

SHUTTER SPEED

Welcome to the world of shutter speed, an essential component of the exposure triangle that empowers photographers to control the very essence of light in their images. Measured in seconds or fractions thereof, it dictates the time your camera's sensor or film is exposed to light.

The shutter mechanism is the unsung hero, choreographing the opening and closing of the camera's eye, determining how long your camera blinks its eye during each shot.

Whether you aim to encapsulate the serenity of a cascading waterfall or the heart-pounding thrill of a racing car, shutter speed captures the raw emotions and pulsating energy of the scenes through the realms of silky trails and freeze frames.

In this section, we'll work through the intricacies of shutter speed, breaking down complex concepts into bite-sized, easily digestible pieces. By the end of this exploration, you'll not only grasp the fundamentals but also wield the knowledge to capture breathtaking aerial photographs.

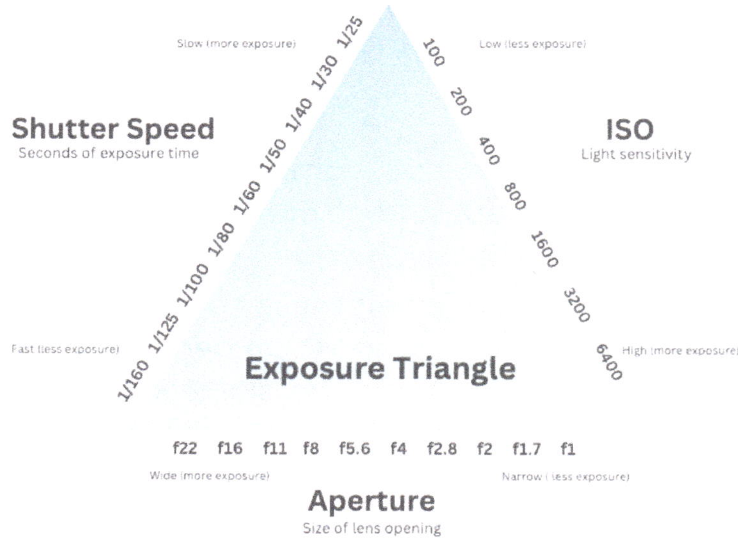

Fast and Slow Shutter Speeds

1. Shutter speed: measured in seconds or fractions thereof akin to the eyelid of a lens blinking open and shut. It dictates the duration during which your camera's sensor is exposed to incoming light. When it is bright you need a faster shutter speed, when it is dark you need a slower shutter speed,

2. Shutter Mechanism: Picture inside the drone camera with gears and mechanisms working in unison. When you push the button to take a photo the button (known as the shutter release) opens, exposing the sensor to incoming light.

3. Fast Shutter Speeds: Imagine freezing time, capturing a speeding bullet mid-flight. Fast shutter speeds, such as 1/1000 or 1/2000 seconds, empower you to do just that. You can freeze fast-moving subjects like speeding cars, mitigating the risk of drone camera shake, and crafting sharp, detailed images that leap off the frame.

1. Motion Blur: Enter the realm of artistic expression with the potential of motion blur. Slow shutter speeds become your brush, allowing you to paint vivid strokes of movement in your stills. This technique infuses energy and fluidity into your aerial images.

4. Slow Shutter Speeds: Now, slow down the world around you with shutter speeds like 1/30 or 1/15 seconds. Unveil the enchantment of introducing intentional motion blur, an artistic choice that imparts a sense of dynamism and grace to your aerial compositions. Slow shutter speeds create effects like light trails or silky waterfalls, crafting dreamy landscapes and introducing an element of time travel to your stills.

Practical Tip: *Embrace slow shutter speeds when photographing cityscapes at night for mesmerising light trails.*

Motion Blur and Freeze Action

2. Freeze Action: Shift gears faster and discover the art of freezing time. Whether it's a hawk in flight, a surfer catching the perfect wave, or a high-speed car, the right shutter speed transforms your drone camera into a time-traveling maestro. Helping you nail that perfect shot, sharp and decisive.

3. Camera Stabilization: But beware, as you use slow shutter speeds, ensuring your drone camera remains steady becomes paramount. In normal shooting camera speeds slower than 1/30 can cause blurred aerial images.

The Best Shutter Speed for DJI Drones

In closing we have found over the last 6 years and through thousands of still images, that the best all round shutter speed on most DJI drones, from under 250 grams with a fixed aperture, to large DJI drones with interchangeable lens cameras and variable apertures, is 1/50 sec.

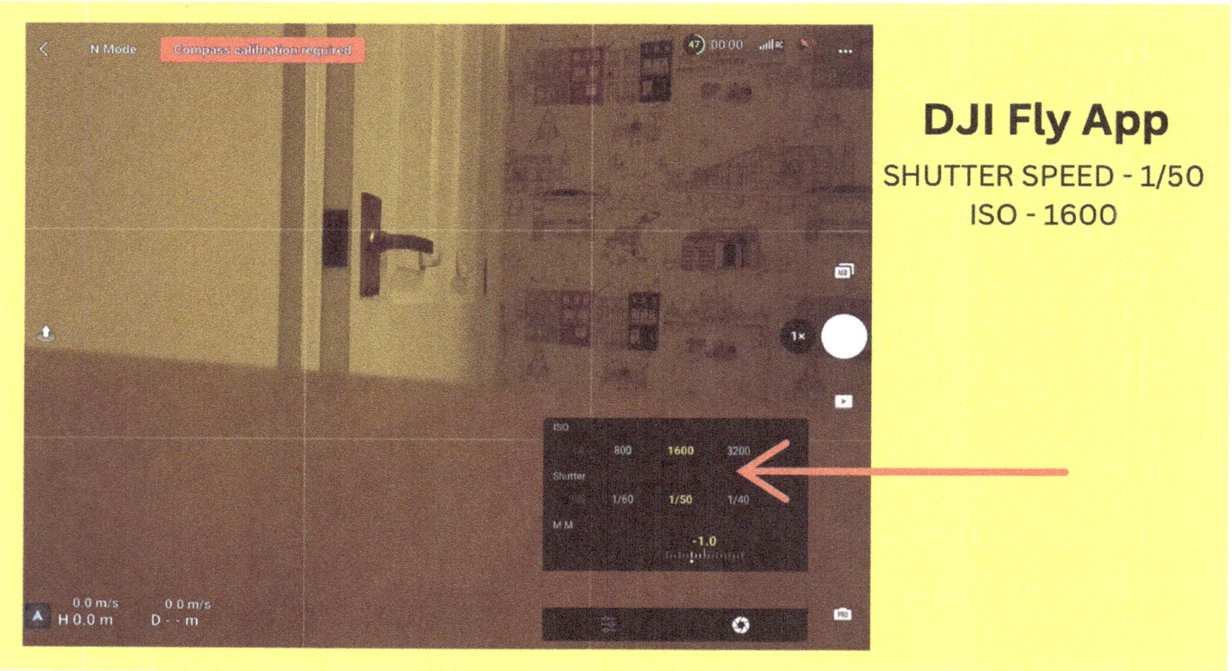

APERTURE

To harness the full potential of your drone's camera, understanding the concept of aperture is essential. In this guide, we will explore aperture, its role in photography, and how it interacts with ISO and shutter speed. Whether you are a beginner or an enthusiast, this guide will provide valuable insights to elevate your skills.

Understanding Aperture

What is Aperture?

Aperture refers to the opening in a camera lens through which light passes to enter the camera body. It is measured in f-stops or f-numbers, and the values represent the size of the aperture opening. The concept of aperture is fundamental to photography, influencing both expcsure and depth of field.

f22   f16   f11   f8   f5.6   f4   f2.8   f2   f1.7   f1

Wide (more exposure)   Narrow (less exposure)

Aperture

Size of lens opening

Aperture Values:

Large Aperture (Small f-number - f1.7): Allows more light to enter the camera.

Small Aperture (Large f-number - f 11): Restricts the amount of light entering the camera.

Role of Aperture in Exposure:

1. Light Control:

Aperture serves as one of the three pillars of exposure control, alongside ISO and shutter speed. By adjusting the aperture, you control the amount of light reaching the camera sensor.

2. Depth of Field:

Aperture significantly impacts depth of field—the range of distance in an image that appears sharp. A large aperture (small f-number) creates a shallow depth of field, isolating subjects from the background, while a small aperture (large f-number) increases depth of field, keeping more elements in focus.

3. Creative Expression:

Aperture is a powerful tool for creative expression. It allows you to control the visual impact of your images by influencing the sharpness of the background and foreground.

Variable Aperture on Some DJI Drones

Now, before you try to change your aperture settings, let's address a small hiccup. Some of our trusty DJI drones do not offer variable aperture settings they are fixed. For example the DJI Mini 3 - f1.7 or DJI Mini 2 - f2.8.

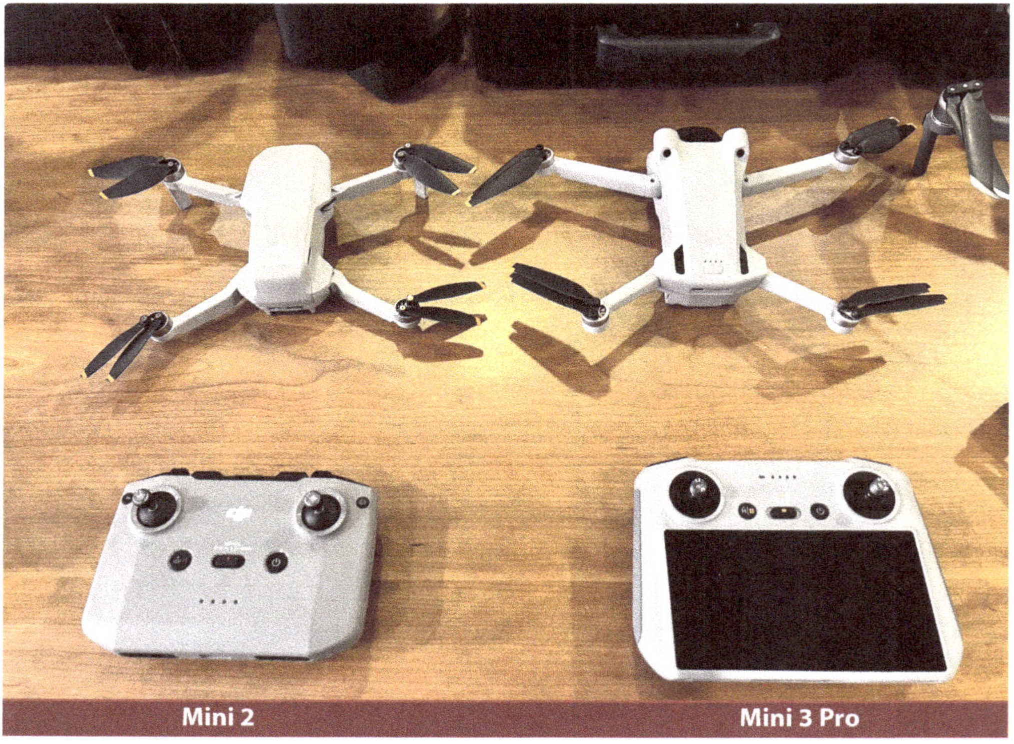

When the aperture adjustment lever is out of your grasp, the exposure triangle becomes your trusty sidekick. Shutter speed and ISO, join hands with ND filters to maintain harmony in your aerial images, ensuring the absence of variable aperture doesn't dim your photographic spirits.

Aperture, ISO, and Shutter Speed: The Exposure Triangle

Understanding the relationship between aperture, ISO, and shutter speed is essential for achieving well-exposed images. These three elements form the exposure triangle, and adjustments to one affects the others.

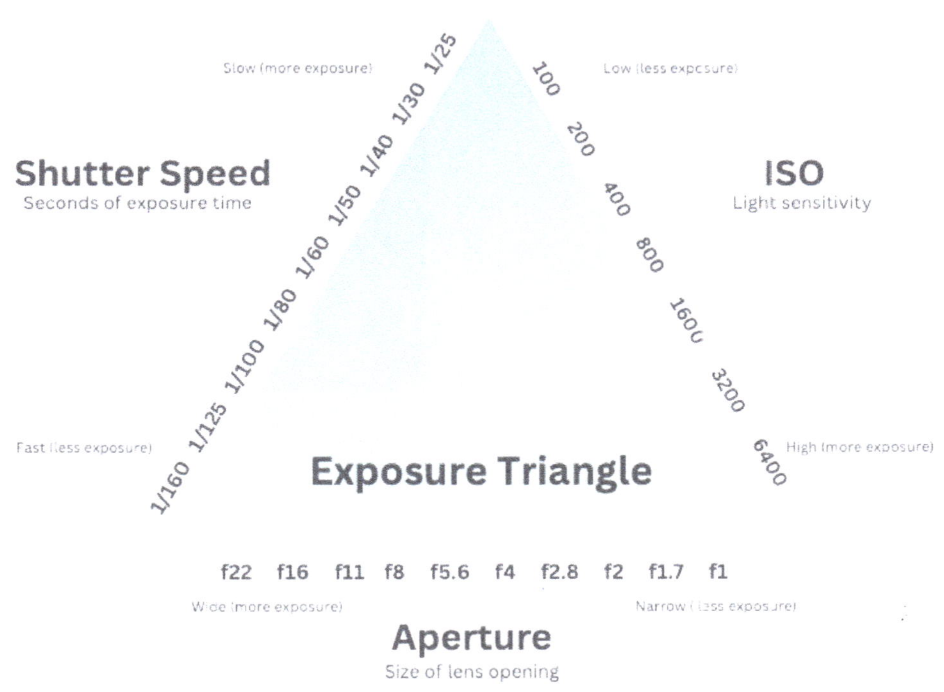

1. Aperture and ISO:

Large Aperture (Small f-number): Allows more light to enter, suitable for low-light conditions. However, it results in a shallower depth of field.

Small Aperture (Large f-number): Restricts light, suitable for bright conditions. It increases depth of field but requires compensating with a slower shutter speed or higher ISO.

ISO (Sensitivity to Light): As aperture influences the amount of light, adjustments may be needed in ISO. A larger aperture (more light) may allow for a lower ISO setting, while a smaller aperture may require a higher ISO setting in low-light situations.

2. Aperture and Shutter Speed:

Large Aperture (Small f-number): Allows more light, but a faster shutter speed may be necessary to prevent overexposure. A faster shutter speed is useful for freezing fast motion.

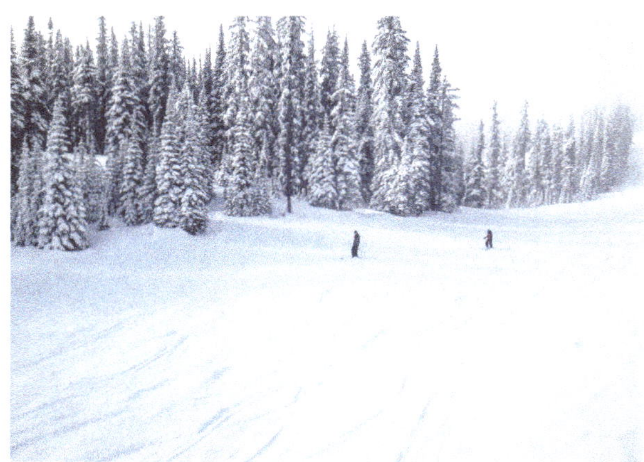
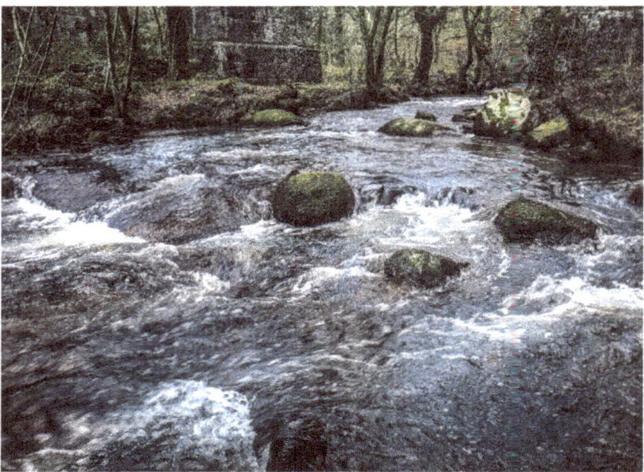

Small Aperture (Large f-number): Restricts light, requiring a slower shutter speed to maintain proper exposure. A slower shutter speed is suitable for capturing motion and long-exposure effects.

Shutter Speed (Duration of Exposure): Adjusting aperture affects the amount of light reaching the sensor, influencing the need for a faster or slower shutter speed. Balancing aperture and shutter speed is crucial for achieving a well-exposed image.

3. Practical Scenarios:

Low-Light Photography: In low-light conditions, a large aperture (small f-number) allows more light, and ISO sensitivity may be adjusted accordingly. However, a balance with shutter speed is crucial to avoid motion blur.

Landscape Photography: For expansive landscapes, a small aperture (large f-number) is preferred to maximize depth of field. ISO can be kept low, and shutter speed adjusted based on the scene's lighting.

Motion Photography: In scenarios involving motion, a faster shutter speed may be required. Adjustments to aperture can compensate for changes in light conditions, ensuring proper exposure.

Choosing the Right Aperture for Drone Photography

1. Depth of Field Considerations:

Large Aperture (Small f-number): Ideal for isolating subjects or emphasizing a specific element in the frame. Suitable for scenarios where a shallow depth of field is desired.

Small Aperture (Large f-number): Perfect for landscape photography, architectural shots, and scenarios where a greater depth of field is crucial to keep multiple elements in focus.

2. Lighting Conditions:

Low Light: In low-light situations, a larger aperture can help capture more light. However, be mindful of the trade-offs in terms of depth of field and potential overexposure.

Bright Conditions: In bright sunlight, a smaller aperture is effective in controlling the amount of light, allowing for well-exposed images with a balanced depth of field

3. Creative Intent:

Blurry Backgrounds: If your goal is to create images with a blurred background, opt for a larger aperture to achieve a shallow depth of field.

Sharp Landscapes: For sharp, detailed landscape shots, choose a smaller aperture to maximize depth of field and ensure focus across the entire scene.

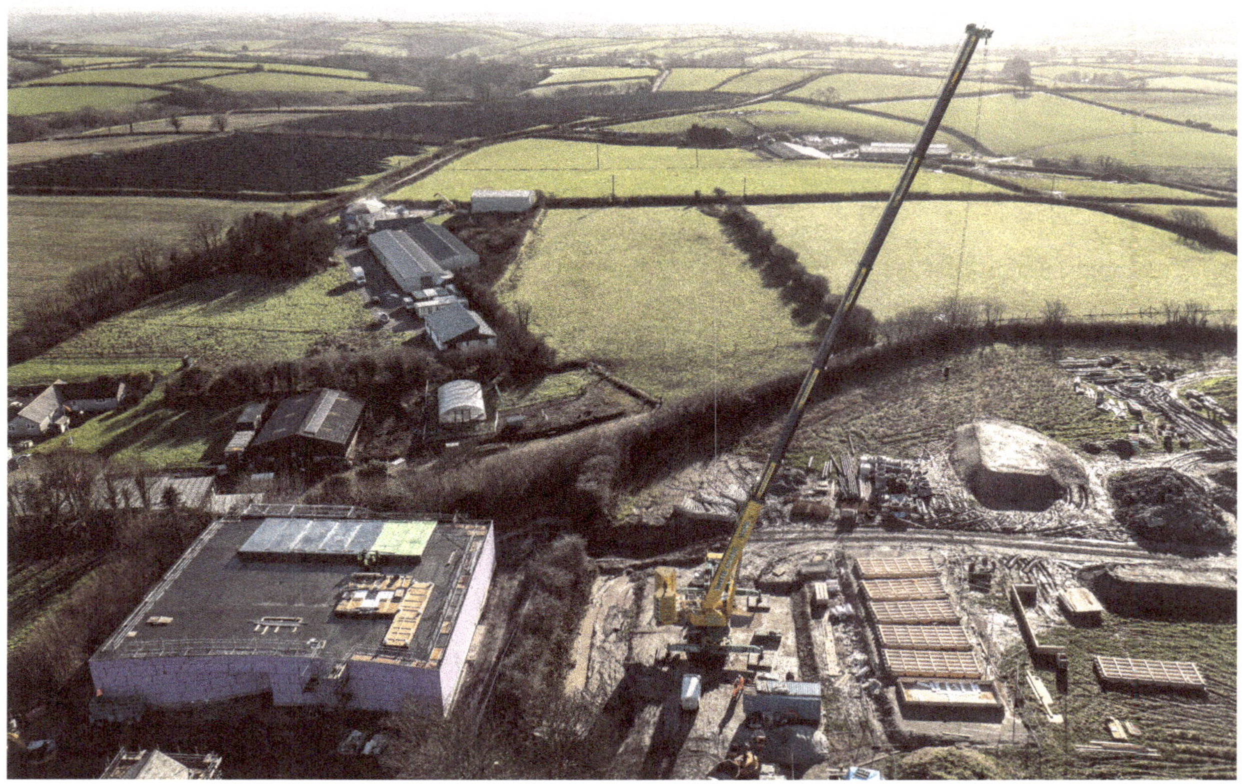

Tips for Implementing Aperture in Drone Photography

1. Experiment with Different Apertures:

Explore the impact of various apertures on your images. Experimenting with both large and small apertures will enhance your understanding of their effects. The aperture sweet spot for most DJI drones is either f4.0 or f5.6.

2. Consider Composition:

Assess your composition and the desired visual impact. Choose an aperture that complements your creative vision and emphasizes the key elements in your frame.

3. Understand the Trade-Offs:

Recognize the trade-offs between aperture, ISO, and shutter speed. Adjustments in one parameter may necessitate changes in the others to maintain proper exposure.

4. Practice Depth of Field Control:

Use aperture to control depth of field intentionally. This skill is particularly valuable for portrait photography, where isolating the subject from the background enhances visual appeal.

5. Adapt to Lighting Conditions:

Be adaptable to changing lighting conditions. Understanding how aperture influences exposure allows you to make real-time adjustments based on the available light.

6. Utilize Aperture Priority Mode:

Many drones offer an Aperture Priority mode, allowing you to set the desired aperture while the camera automatically adjusts the shutter speed for proper exposure. This mode is useful for those transitioning from automatic to manual settings.

Mastering aperture in drone photography is a journey that combines technical understanding with creative expression. You should embrace the interplay between aperture, ISO, and shutter speed empowering you to confidently capture stunning aerial images. Whether you aim to create dreamy portraits, sharp landscapes, or experiment with long exposure effects, a solid grasp of aperture is your key to unlocking the full potential of drone photography.

As you embark on your drone photography adventures, remember that practice is fundamental to mastery. Experiment with different apertures, observe their effects on your images, and adapt your techniques based on the unique challenges and opportunities presented by aerial photography. With each flight, you'll refine your skills and develop an intuitive understanding. In the metadata of each image it will give you the key information including the aperture you selected for the photo.

ISO

 ISO, or the International Organization for Standardisation, might sound like a bureaucratic entity, but in the world of aerial photography, it's the magician behind the curtain of exposure. In this section, we're diving deep into the world of sensitivity, exploring low and high ISO, mastering the delicate dance of the exposure triangle, and banishing the notorious noise that can haunt our photographs.

Cracking the ISO Code: A Beginner's Guide

Let's start our exploration with the fundamental question: What is ISO? At its core, ISO measures how sensitive your camera's sensor is to light. Picture it as a dimmer switch, controlling the brightness of your photographs.

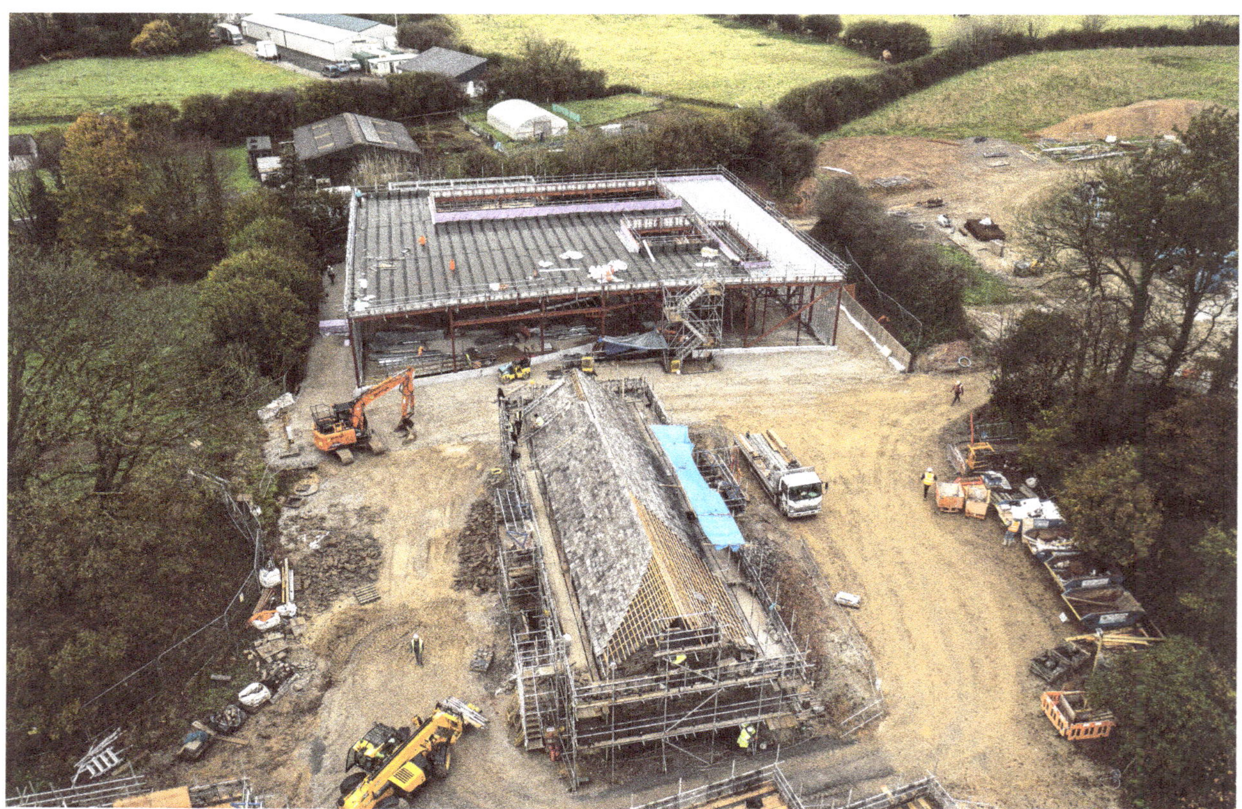

The sweet spot for ISO on most DJI drone camera is 100 in normal light.

1. Low ISO: Let There Be Light (but Not Too Much): Low ISO settings, like ISO 100 or 200, are the Zen masters of sensitivity. They produce images with minimal noise, creating crisp, clean shots that bask in the glory of well-lit situations. It's like bathing your images in soft, natural light, resulting in optimal image quality.

2. High ISO: Illuminating the Shadows: Now, enter the high ISO settings – ISO 800, 1600, or even higher to 6400. These settings become your trusty sidekick in the dark of low-light scenarios. They crank up the sensitivity, allowing your camera to capture images in situations where mere mortals would struggle to see. But beware – with great sensitivity comes great responsibility. High ISO can introduce noise, the gremlin of photography.

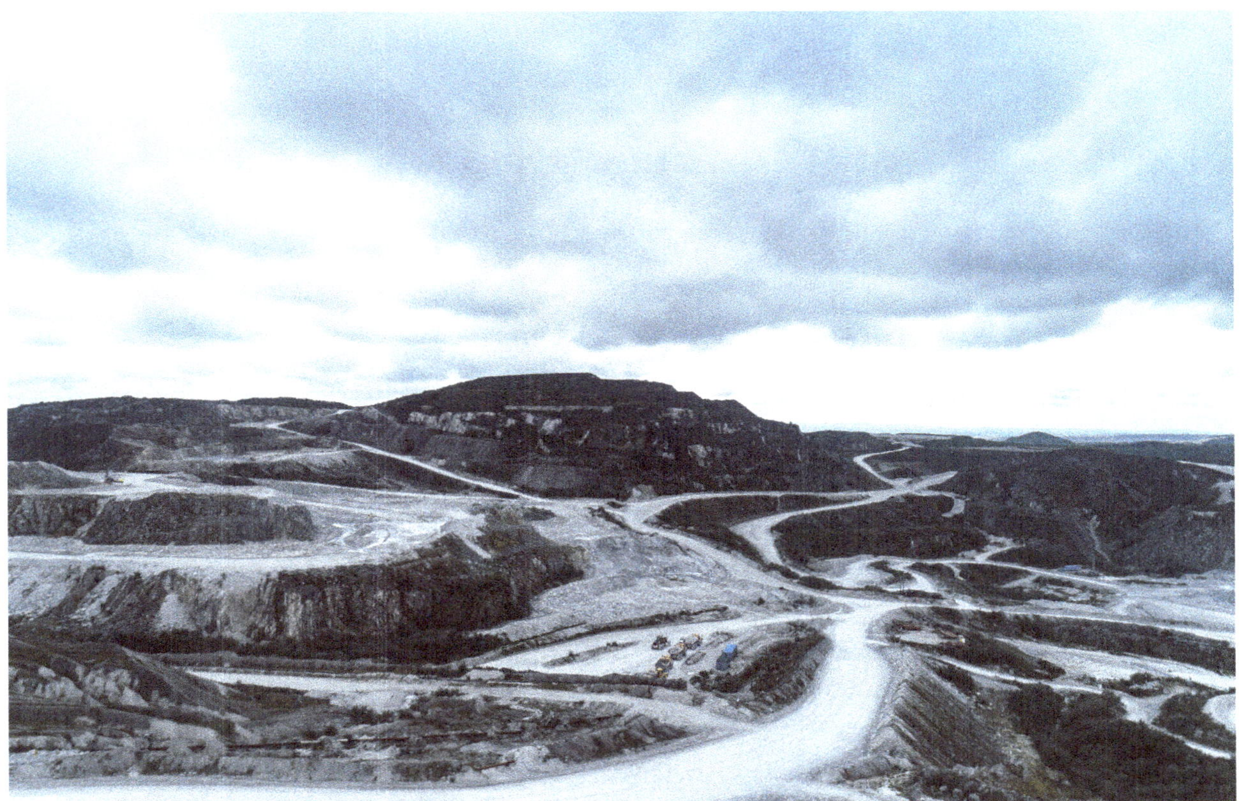

ISO, Aperture, Shutter Speed

Now, let's revisit the exposure triangle, that dynamic dance of ISO, aperture, and shutter speed. Picture it as a trio of performers, each playing a vital role in creating the perfect photographic harmony.

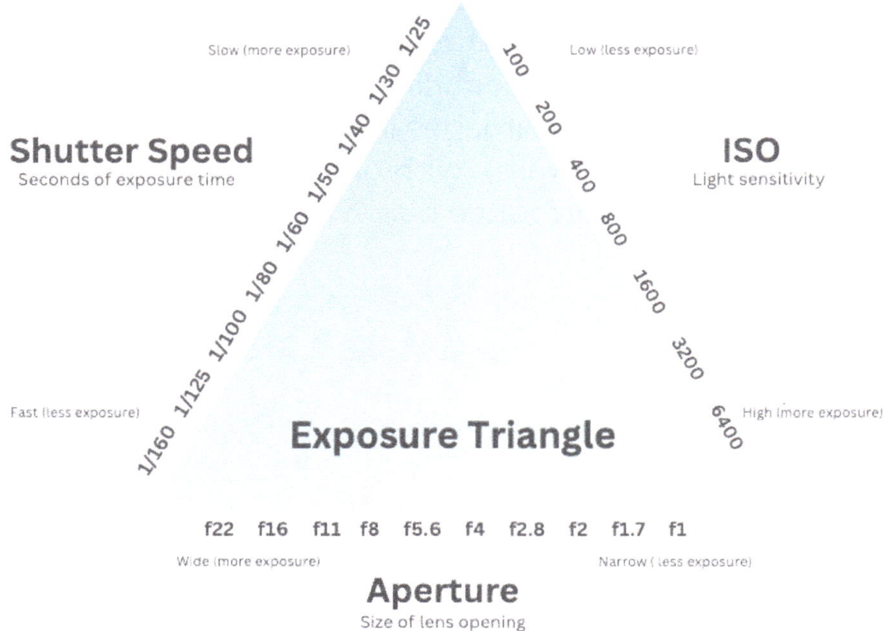

1. ISO as the Illuminator: ISO is like the lighting director, controlling the sensitivity of your camera's sensor. When the stage is too dark, increase ISO to brighten the scene. Conversely, when the spotlight is too intense, dial down ISO for a more controlled exposure. Understanding this interaction is key to capturing the perfect aerial scene.

2. Using ISO to Adjust Exposure: There are times when adjusting aperture or shutter speed alone won't cut it. Here's where ISO comes in. If your scene is too dark, bump up the ISO for a brighter exposure. Need more light on a gloomy day? Bump up the ISO. Shooting in bright sunlight? Bring it down a notch. It's your secret weapon for fine-tuning exposure in diverse lighting conditions. It's like having a dimmer switch for the lights on your aerial stage.

Noise: Uninvited Guest at the Exposure Party

It's the unwanted graininess or speckles that can infiltrate your images, especially at high ISO settings. But fear not, for understanding the enemy is the first step to conquering it.

1. Recognizing Noise: You can see those speckles that turn your smooth skies into a pixelated nightmare. To remove it you need to adjust the other two sides of the exposure triangle. The scale of the noise will also depend on the drone camera you are using. Most drone cameras show unacceptable noise above ISO 1600.

2. Maximizing Image Quality: The quest for the perfect aerial photograph is not just about capturing light; it's about capturing it with finesse. On the DJI Mavic 3 Pro and Mini 4 Pro they have a night mode in the App settings which allows you to use very high ISO setting and maximize image quality while keeping noise in check. Think of it as finding the sweet spot between sensitivity and serenity.

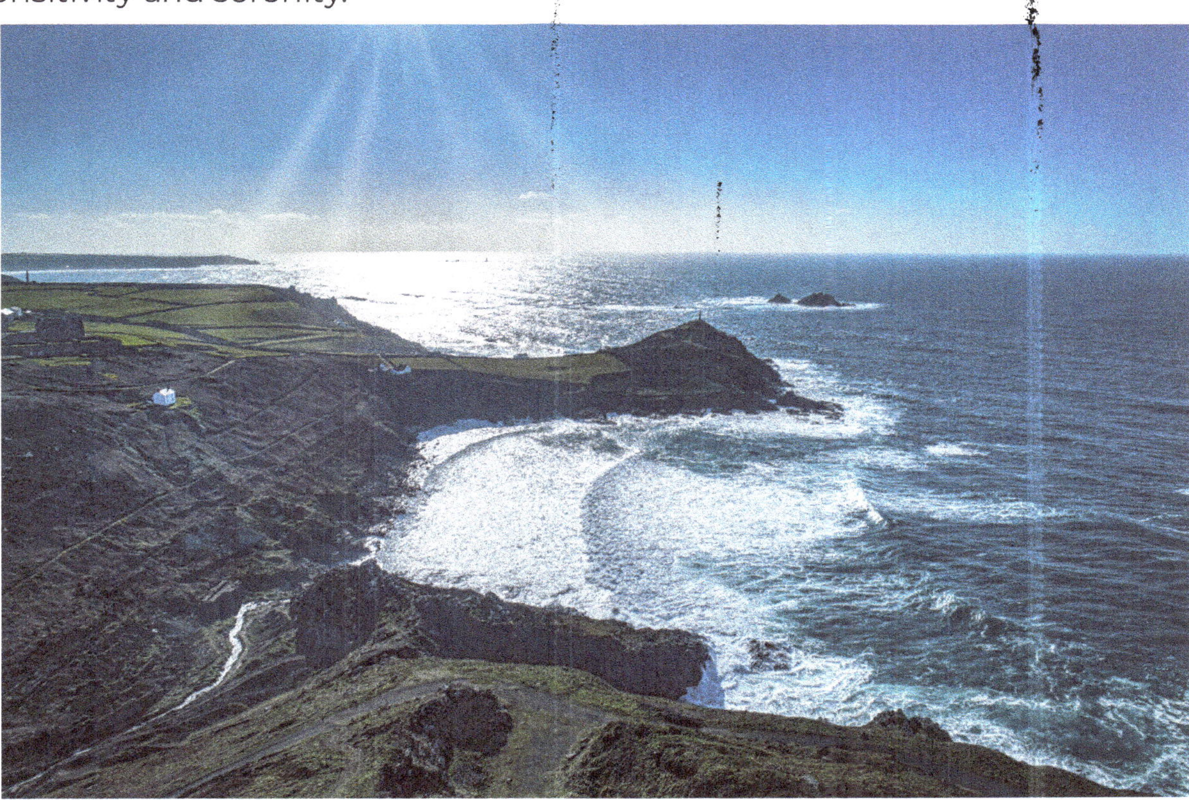

Aerial Adventures with ISO: The Final Act

Now that you're armed with the knowledge of ISO sensitivity, the exposure triangle, and the ever-elusive noise, it's time to take your ISO mastery to the skies.

Revisit these pages, let the concepts twirl in your mind, ISO isn't just technical jargon, it's your artistic ally. Experiment with different ISO settings, practice with purpose, and make ISO your ally in the vast expanse of aerial photography.

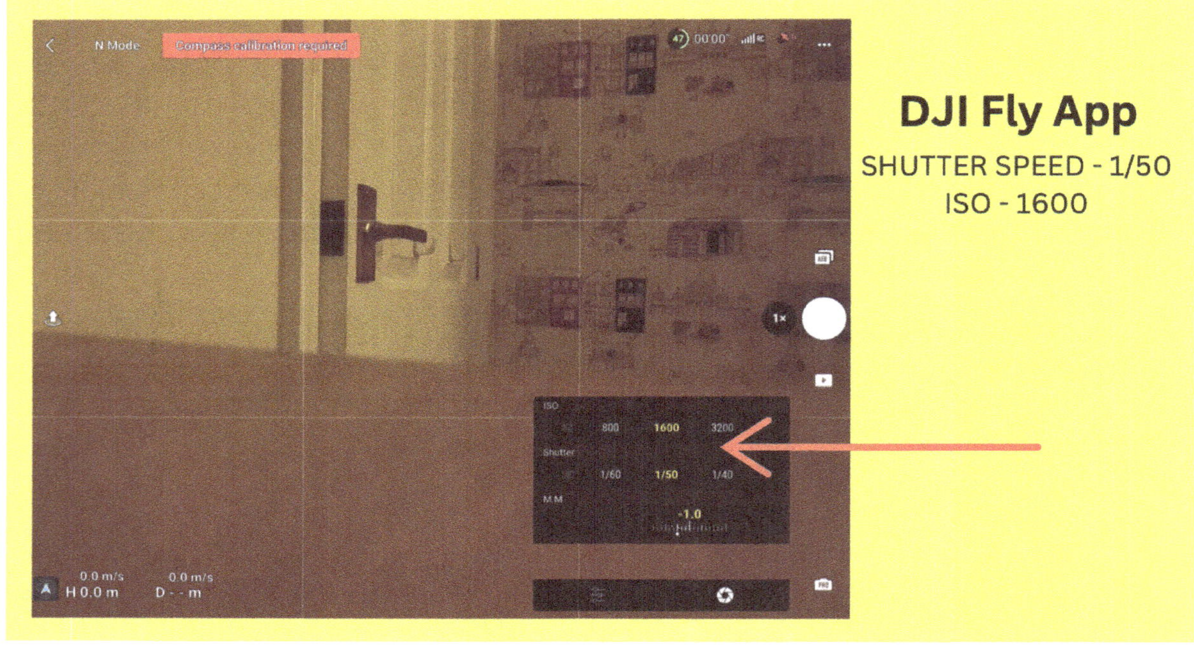

DYNAMIC RANGE

Dynamic range is a fundamental concept in photography that plays a crucial role in capturing and reproducing the full spectrum of light in a scene. Understanding dynamic range is essential for making informed decisions about exposure, post-processing, and achieving images that accurately reflect the visual richness of a scene. In this guide, we will explore the concept of dynamic range, its significance in drone photography, and how techniques like Auto Exposure Bracketing (AEB) and High Dynamic Range (HDR) photography can be employed to enhance image quality.

What is Dynamic Range

Dynamic range refers to the range of tones from the darkest to the brightest in a given image or scene. In photography, it is often expressed in stops of light and is a critical factor in determining the level of detail that can be captured, especially in high-contrast scenes where there are both deep shadows and bright highlights.

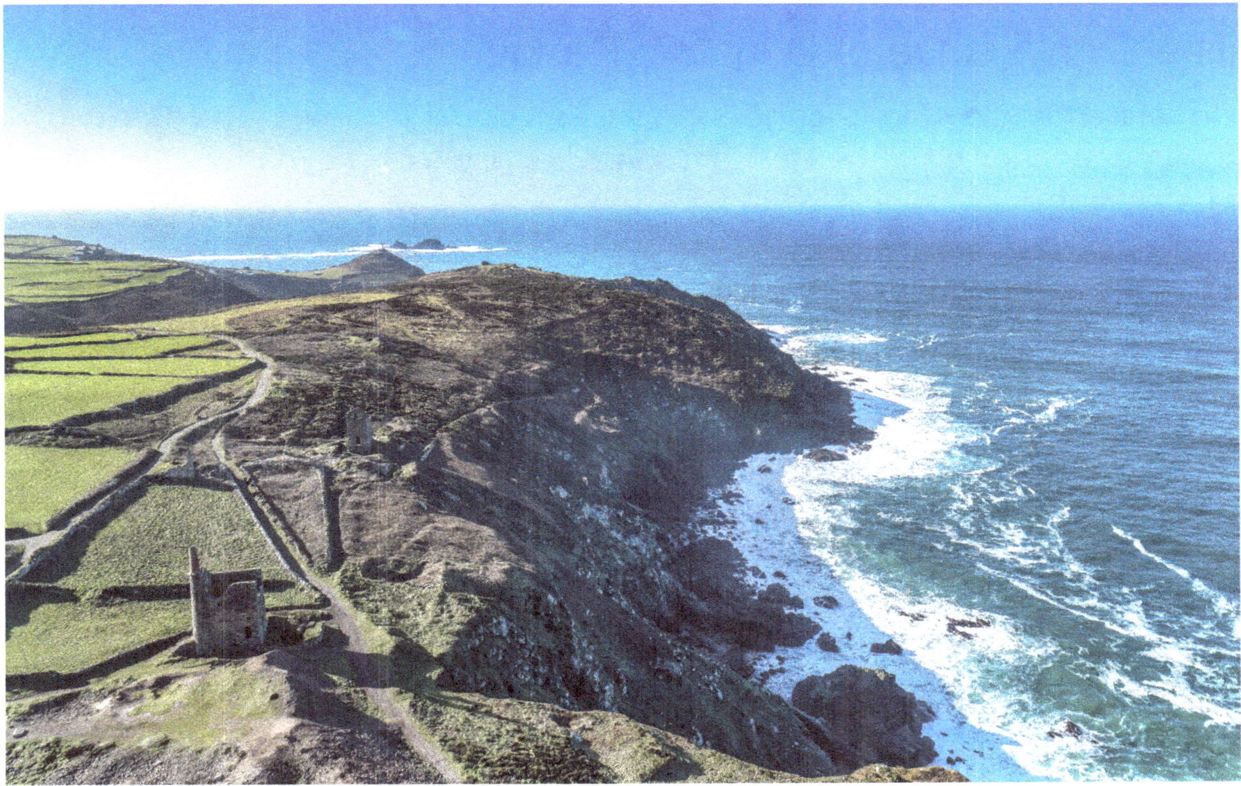

Components of Dynamic Range:

1. Shadows:

The darkest areas of an image, where minimal light is reflected or captured by the camera sensor.

2. Midtones:

The tones between shadows and highlights, representing the average brightness levels in a scene.

3. Highlights:

The brightest areas of an image, where the most light is reflected or captured by the camera sensor.

A drone camera with a wide dynamic range can capture details in both shadow and highlight areas, resulting in a well-balanced and visually appealing photograph.

The Significance of Dynamic Range

Understanding dynamic range is crucial, as it directly impacts the quality of the images they produce. Here are some key aspects of dynamic range in photography:

1. Contrast and Detail: A broader dynamic range allows for the capture of more details in both shadow and highlight areas. This is particularly important in scenes with high contrast, such as landscapes with bright skies and dark foregrounds.

2. Exposure Control: Dynamic range influences the photographer's ability to control exposure. A camera with a wide dynamic range provides more flexibility in choosing exposure settings without losing critical details.

3. Post-Processing: When working with RAW files, which retain a higher dynamic range compared to JPEGs, you have greater flexibility during post-processing. This allows for adjustments to exposure, contrast, and highlights and shadows without compromising image quality.

4. Low-Light Performance: Dynamic range is crucial in low-light situations. A camera with good dynamic range can capture details in the shadows without introducing excessive noise.

5. HDR Photography: High Dynamic Range (HDR) photography, a technique we will delve into shortly, leverages the camera's dynamic range to capture and merge multiple exposures, creating a final image with a broader tonal range.

Auto Exposure Bracketing (AEB)

Auto Exposure Bracketing (AEB) is a feature found in many drone cameras that allows you to automatically capture a series of images at different exposure levels. AEB is a valuable tool for situations where the dynamic range of a scene exceeds the camera's capabilities to capture details in both shadows and highlights in a single exposure.

How AEB Works:

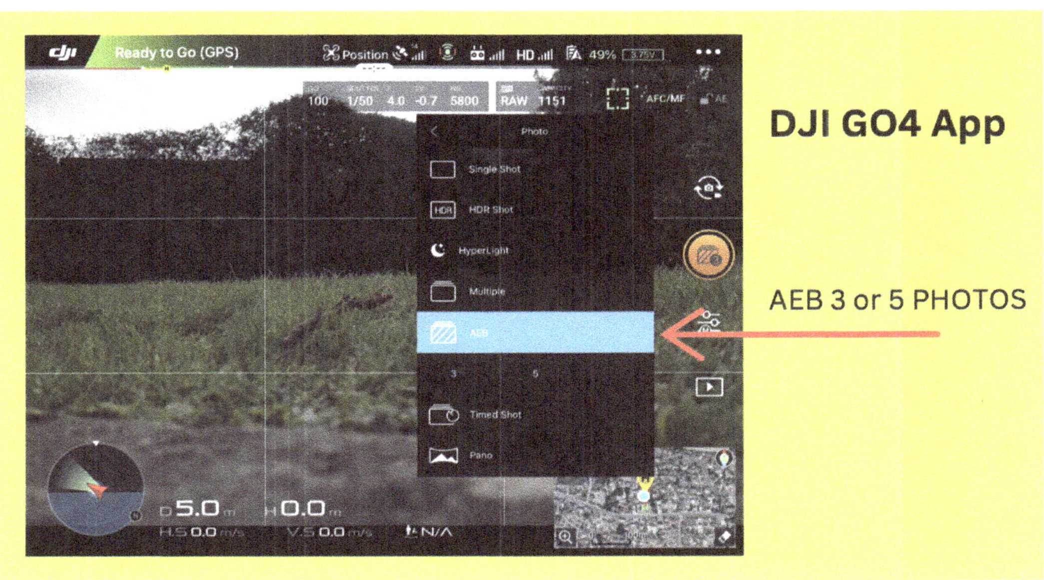

1. Set Exposure Bracketing: In the camera settings, you selects the number of frames (3 or 5) to be captured and the exposure increment between each frame.

2. Capture Multiple Exposures: When the shutter button is pressed, the camera takes a sequence of shots, each with a different exposure. The exposures typically include one at the metered exposure, one underexposed, and one overexposed.

3. Post-Processing: The photographer can later choose the best-exposed image or merge the multiple exposures during post-processing to create an HDR image.

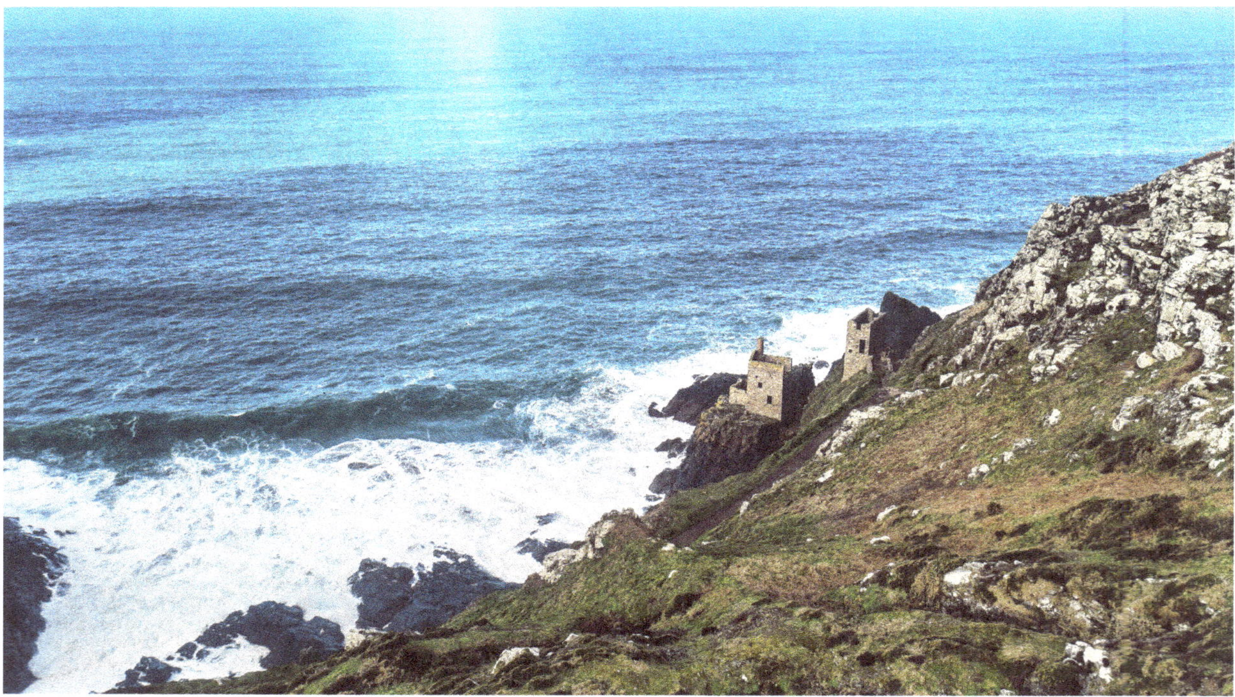

Advantages of AEB:

1. Increased Dynamic Range: AEB allows photographers to capture a broader dynamic range by including details from both shadow and highlight areas.

2. Flexible Exposure Control: It provides flexibility in choosing the best exposure during post-processing without the risk of losing critical details in highlights or shadows.

3. HDR Photography Preparation: AEB sets the foundation for HDR photography by providing the necessary bracketed exposures for merging into a single HDR image.

High Dynamic Range (HDR)

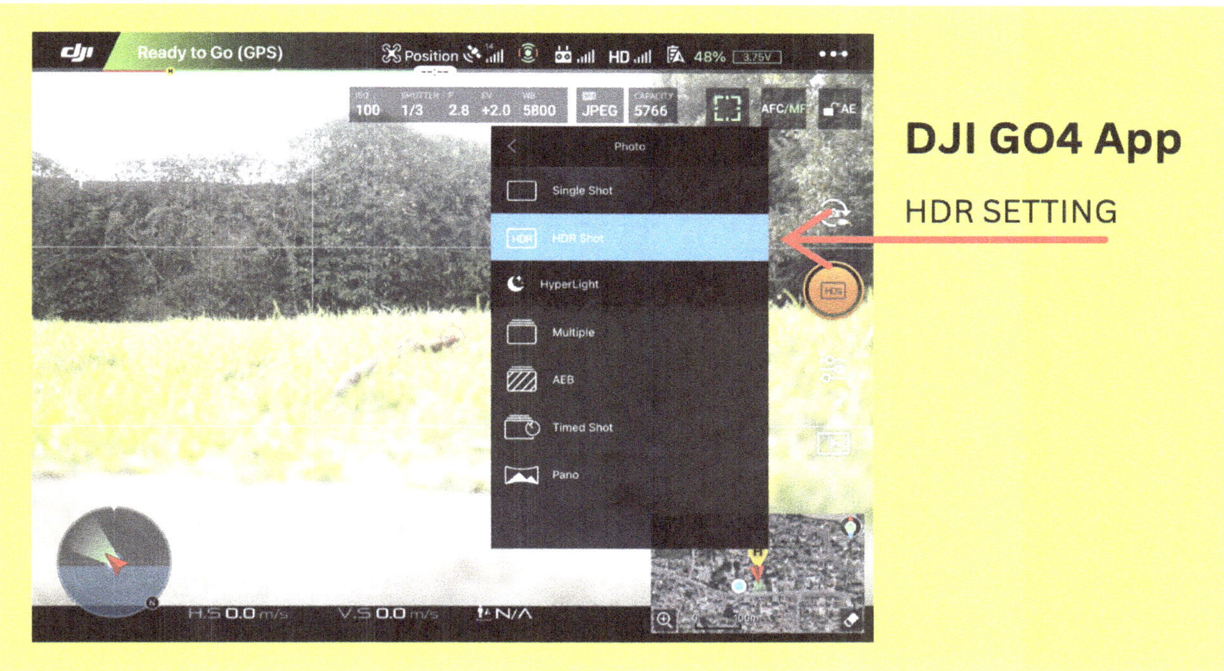

HDR photography is a technique that involves capturing multiple exposures of a scene and merging them to create a final image with a more extensive dynamic range than a single exposure would allow.

Steps to Create an HDR Image:

1. Capture AEB Sequences: Use AEB to capture a series of bracketed exposures, typically including one properly exposed frame, one underexposed frame, and one overexposed frame.

2. Image Alignment: To ensure precise alignment of the images, especially in handheld situations, use software or in-camera stabilization to match the frames.

3. Merging Exposures: Utilize HDR software or post-processing tools to merge the bracketed exposures into a single image. The software combines the details from each exposure, creating a final image with an extended tonal range.

4. Merging Exposures: During the merging process, tone mapping is applied to distribute the tonal values in a visually appealing way. This step enhances the overall dynamic range of the image.

Advantages of HDR Photography:

1. Enhanced Dynamic Range: HDR photography allows for the capture and presentation of a broader dynamic range in the final image.

 2. Detail Preservation: By combining exposures, HDR retains details in both shadow and highlight areas, providing a more comprehensive representation of the scene.

3. Artistic Expression: HDR techniques enable photographers to create visually striking and artistic images, especially in situations with challenging lighting conditions.

4. Realism in Photography: HDR can be used to create images that closely resemble the way the human eye perceives a scene, making it a powerful tool for realistic and natural-looking photographs.

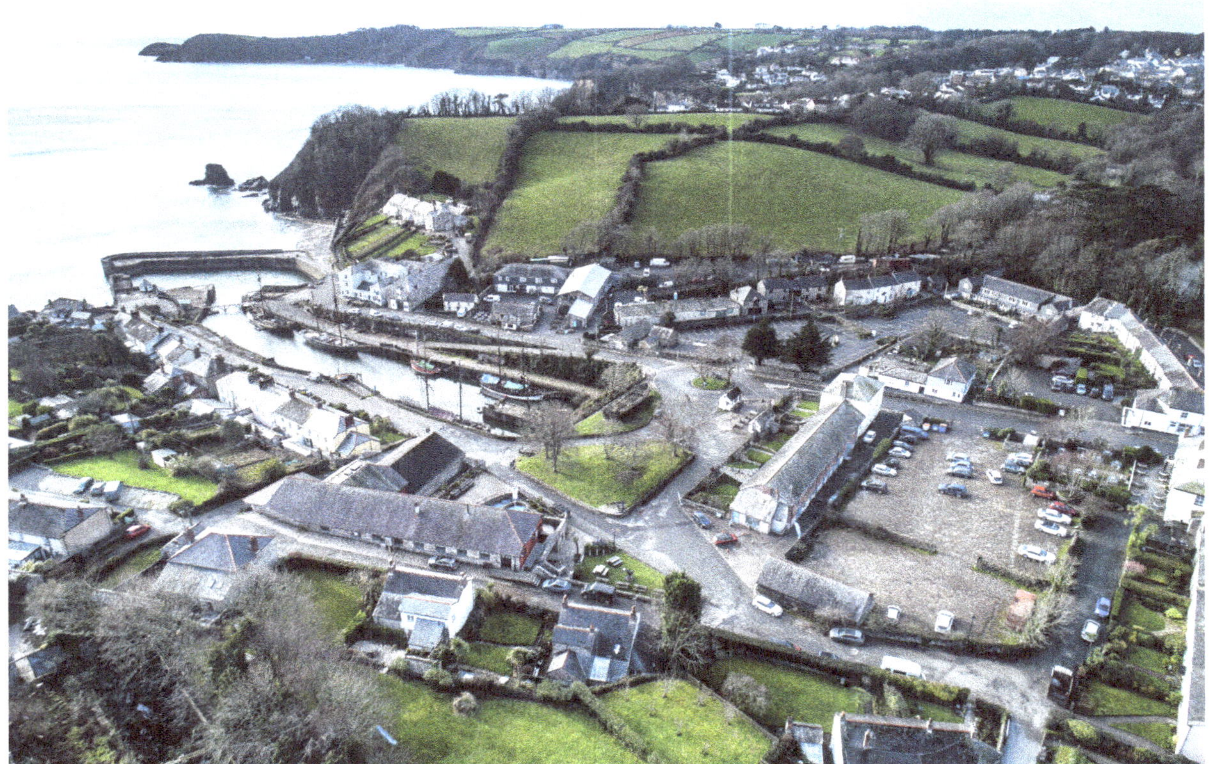

Conclusion

Dynamic range is a critical aspect of drone photography that directly influences the quality and visual impact of your images. Grasp the concept of dynamic range, its components (shadows, midtones, and highlights), and how it affects exposure and post-processing decisions.

Auto Exposure Bracketing (AEB) is a valuable tool that extends the drone camera's capabilities in capturing a broader dynamic range. It provides you with the flexibility to choose the best exposure during post-processing and serves as the foundation for High Dynamic Range (HDR) photography.

HDR photography, when executed thoughtfully, allows photographers to create images with enhanced dynamic range, preserving details in challenging lighting conditions. It opens up new possibilities for artistic expression and provides a tool for capturing scenes that may be difficult to represent accurately in a single exposure.

Embark on their learning journey, mastering dynamic range, AEB, and HDR photography will significantly contribute to their ability to capture stunning and impactful images. Experimenting with these techniques and understanding their applications will empower you to expand their creative horizons and produce photographs that stand out in terms of both technical excellence and visual appeal.

OTHER CAMERA SETTINGS

White Balance & Sharpness

Both headings should be set manually in the DJI Go4 or Fly app before you start to fly. They can be found on the same app subheading

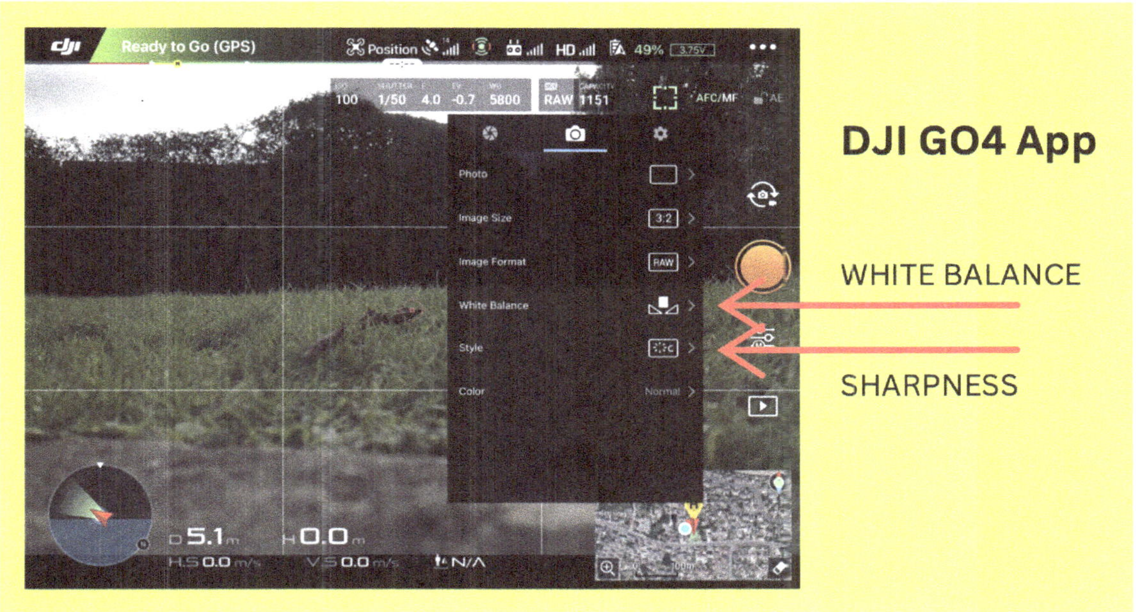

White Balance

White balance is the adjustment of colors in your images to ensure that whites appear truly white under different lighting conditions. Aerial photography encounters a wide range of lighting scenarios, from the warm tones of sunrise to the cool hues of a cloudy day. Understanding and adjusting the white balance settings on your drone's camera will help you achieve accurate color reproduction.

The white balance can be left on auto, but for the best result it is better to set the white balance on your drone manually. The manual range for you to set is from 5,000 to 6,400k (k = kelvin) A Dull day is 5,300k, normal daylight 5,900k, and very bright sunlight 6,400k

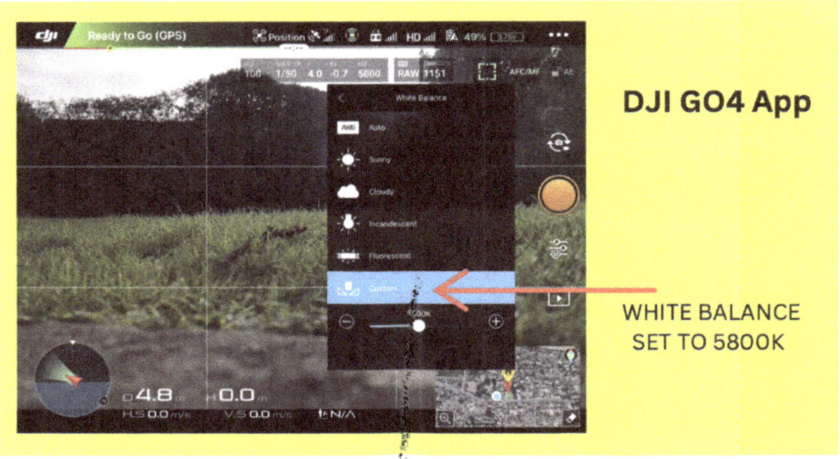

Sharpness

The default setting for sharpness in most DJI drones is too sharp so we recommend you reduce the sharpness by -2 before you fly. It can always be sharpened in post production editing. The sharpness setting can be found under the Style tab in the app and sharpness is indicated by the triangle symbol.

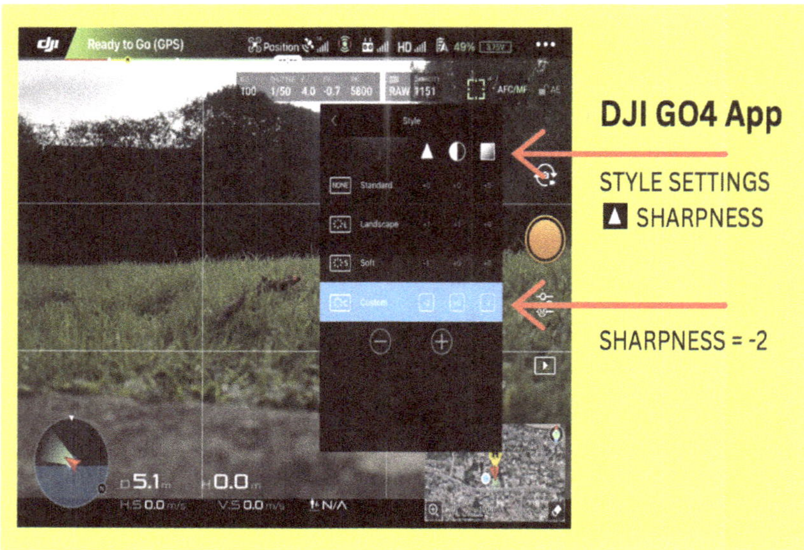

EV - Exposure Compensation Value

Exposure Compensation Value (EV) allows you to make small adjustments to the brightness or darkness of their images. Drone cameras automatically calculate exposure based on the available light, but challenging lighting conditions, such as high contrast scenes, may require manual adjustments.

Positive EV values increase exposure, suitable for scenes with shadows, while negative values decrease exposure, useful for bright, high-key environments. EV enables photographers to make small adjustments to maintain proper exposure, revealing details in both highlights and shadows. Use the histogram for feedback to fine tune your exposure.

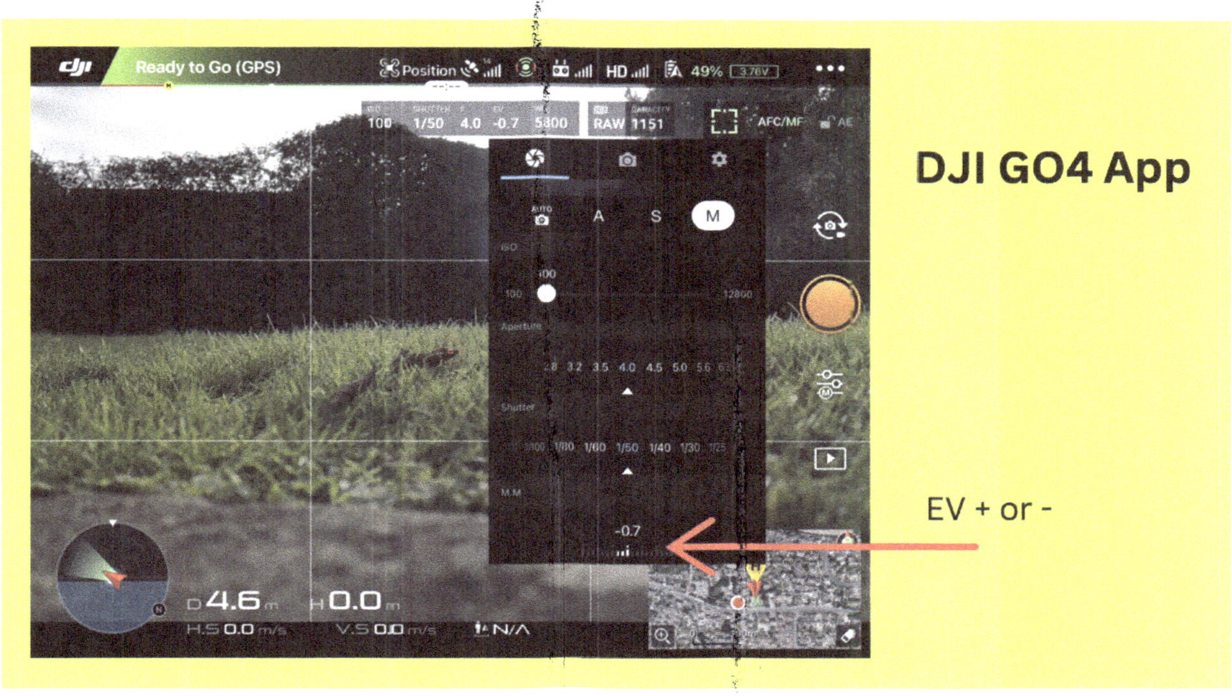

IMAGE FORMATS

There are two format you can shoot in JPEG and RAW. With most DJI drones you can shoot in ether JPEG or RAW. There is a selection option in the app. Sometimes on the cheaper smaller drones the selection option is only JPEG or JPEG and RAW. If you select JPEG and RAW it will store two images on your SD card – one image in JPEG and one image in RAW.

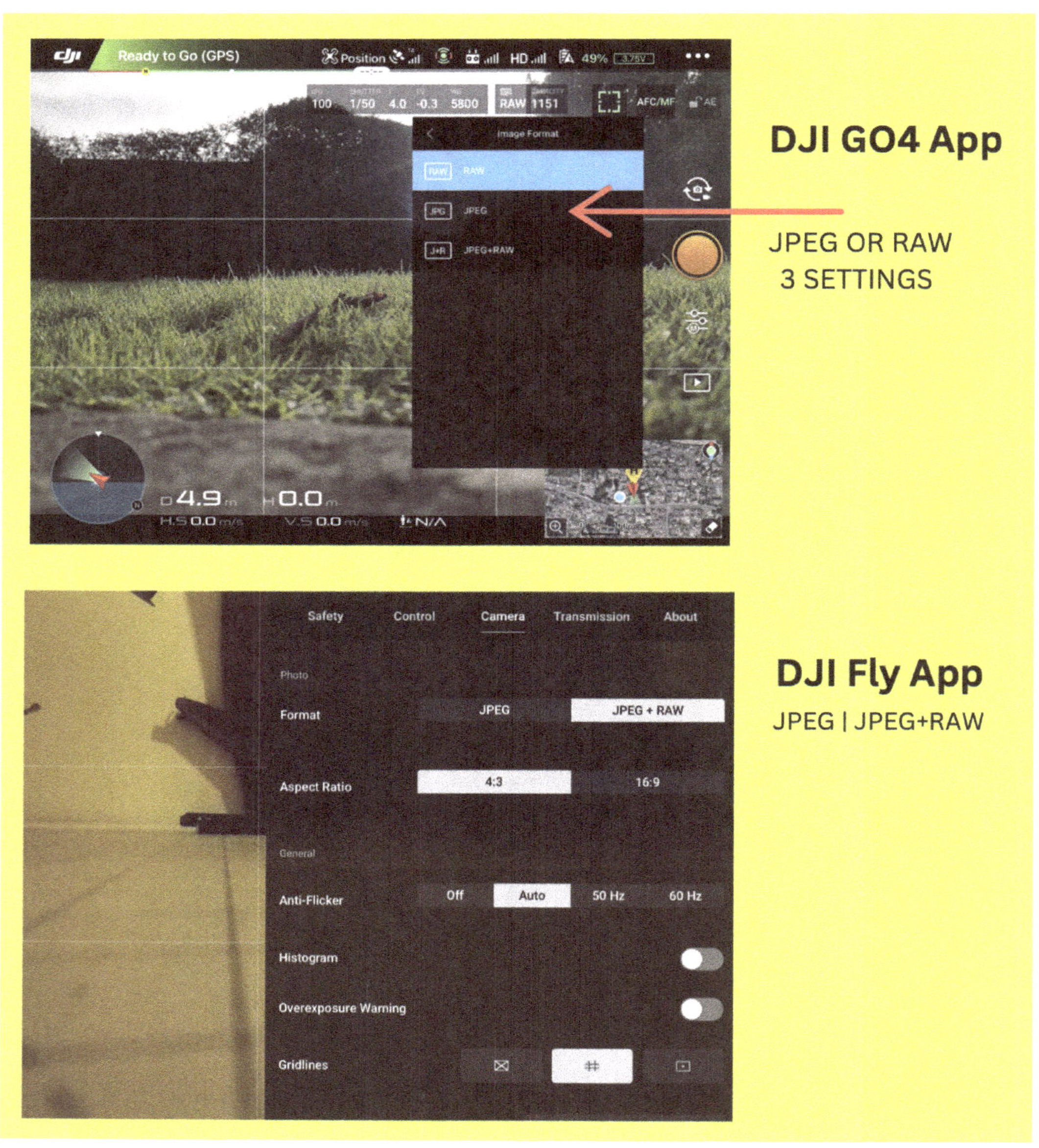

Understanding the differences between these two formats is important for you to make informed decisions about your shooting preferences and post-processing workflow.

What is JPEG?

JPEG is a widely used image compression format that employs something called lossy compression, meaning that some data is discarded during the compression process to reduce file size. This format was developed by the Joint Photographic Experts Group, leading to its acronym, and it has become the standard for sharing and displaying images across various devices and platforms.

Characteristics of JPEG:

1. Compression:

JPEG uses lossy compression to reduce file size. This compression results in a smaller file but sacrifices some image data, leading to a potential loss of detail and quality.

2. File Size:

JPEG files are significantly smaller compared to RAW files. This makes them more suitable for situations where storage space is a concern, and quick sharing or uploading of images is necessary.

3. Processing:

JPEG files undergo in-camera processing, where the camera applies settings such as white balance, sharpness, and colour saturation. This means that the photographer has less control over these aspects during post-processing.

4. Colour Space:

JPEG files use the sRGB colour space, which is the standard for most digital displays. While suitable for online sharing and printing, it may have limitations in capturing the full spectrum of colours compared to RAW.

5. Editing Limitations:

Due to the lossy compression, JPEG files have limited flexibility for extensive post-processing. Adjusting exposure or correcting white balance may lead to a quicker degradation of image quality compared to RAW.

When to Use JPEG:

Everyday Photography: JPEG is ideal for everyday photography where convenience, quick sharing, and smaller file sizes are priorities. This includes casual photography, social media sharing, and events.

Limited Post-processing: If minimal post-processing is anticipated, such as when the in-camera settings adequately capture the desired look, shooting in JPEG is efficient.

Storage Constraints: In situations where storage space is limited, shooting in JPEG allows for capturing a large number of images without quickly filling up memory cards.

What is RAW?

RAW is a file format that preserves all the original data captured by the camera's sensor without any in-camera processing. Unlike JPEG, RAW is an uncompressed digital negative and retains maximum detail and dynamic range, providing photographers with greater flexibility during post-processing.

Characteristics of RAW:

1. No Compression:

RAW files are uncompressed, retaining all the data captured by the camera's sensor. This results in larger file sizes but ensures maximum image quality.

2. File Size:

RAW files are significantly larger than their JPEG counterparts due to the absence of compression (two to six times larger than JPEG). This allows for extensive post-processing without a significant loss of image quality.

3. Processing Control:

RAW files provide you with complete control over post-processing parameters such as white balance, exposure, contrast, and sharpness. This allows for fine-tuning and correction of various aspects during editing.

4. Colour Space:

Unlike JPEG, RAW files are not limited to a specific colour space. They can be processed and exported in various colour spaces, including Adobe RGB, which has a broader colour gamut.

5. Editing Flexibility:

RAW files offer unparalleled editing flexibility. You can make significant adjustments to exposure, recover details in shadows and highlights, and apply non-destructive edits without compromising image quality.

When to Use RAW:

Professional Photography: RAW is preferred in professional settings where maximum image quality and control over post-processing are essential. This includes commercial photography, portrait sessions, and studio work.

Extensive Post-processing: If you plan to perform extensive post-processing, such as exposure adjustments, colour grading, and advanced retouching, shooting in RAW provides the necessary flexibility.

High Dynamic Range Scenes: In scenes with challenging lighting conditions and a wide dynamic range, RAW allows for better recovery of details in both highlights and shadows.

Colour Critical Work: For projects where colour accuracy is paramount, such as product photography or print publications, RAW provides the ability to fine-tune colour reproduction.

Choice Between JPEG or RAW

The choice between shooting in JPEG or RAW depends on various factors, and there is no one-size-fits-all answer. Photographers often find themselves making this decision based on the specific requirements of a given situation.

JPEG is well-suited for scenarios where smaller file sizes, quick sharing, and minimal post-processing are priorities. It is the go-to format for casual photography, events, and situations where storage space is limited.

On the other hand, RAW is the preferred choice when maximum image quality, editing flexibility, and control over post-processing are crucial. Professional photographers, commercial work, and situations with challenging lighting conditions benefit greatly from the advantages of shooting in RAW.

RAW files are between two and six times bigger than JPEG files without any compression. RAW files are in a 14-bit channel with 16384 levels of brightness and JPEG are in a 8 bit channel with only 256 levels of brightness. This high dynamic range gives RAW a massive advantage over JPEG.

DRONE PHOTOGRAPHY TECHNIQUES

In the world of aerial photography, understanding the nuances of lighting conditions is pivotal. The golden hour, blue hour, and long exposure techniques can elevate your drone photography to new heights. In this guide, we'll delve into the magic of the golden and blue hours, explore their variations across seasons, and unravel the secrets of long exposure photography with the aid of ND filters.

The Golden Hour: A Time of Enchanting Light

The golden hour, often referred to as the magic hour, is a brief yet magical period shortly after sunrise or before sunset. During this time, the sun casts a warm and soft glow, creating long shadows and adding a golden hue to the landscape. For drone photographers, the golden hour is a prime opportunity to capture stunning, ethereal imagery.

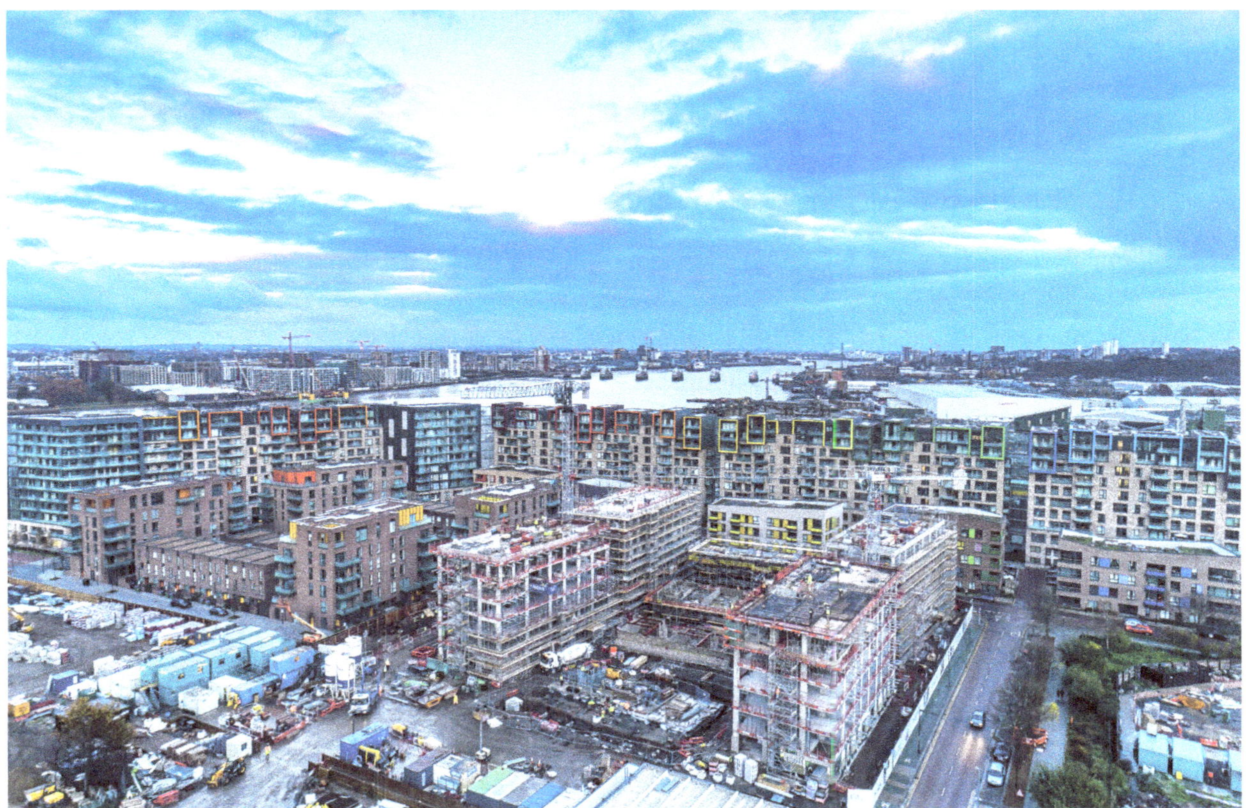

Characteristics of the Golden Hour:

1. Soft, Warm Light:

The sun's angle during the golden hour results in soft, diffused light that enhances colours and textures without harsh shadows.

2. Long Shadows:

The low angle of the sun creates elongated shadows, adding depth and dimension to landscapes and subjects.

3. Warm Colour Palette:

The golden hour bathes the surroundings in warm tones, ranging from soft yellows to rich oranges and reds.

4. Enhanced Textures:

The low-angle light accentuates textures, bringing out details in landscapes, buildings, and natural elements.

Golden Hour Timing:

Summer: The golden hour occurs shortly after sunrise and before sunset, typically lasting around 1-2 hours.

Winter: The golden hour is relatively shorter, lasting around 30 minutes to an hour after sunrise and before sunset.

The Blue Hour: A Tranquil Twilight Period

The blue hour is a captivating period that occurs before sunrise and after sunset when the sun is just below the horizon. During this time, the sky takes on a deep blue hue, creating a serene and enchanting atmosphere. For drone photographers, the blue hour offers a unique canvas to capture mesmerizing images with a different mood compared to the golden hour.

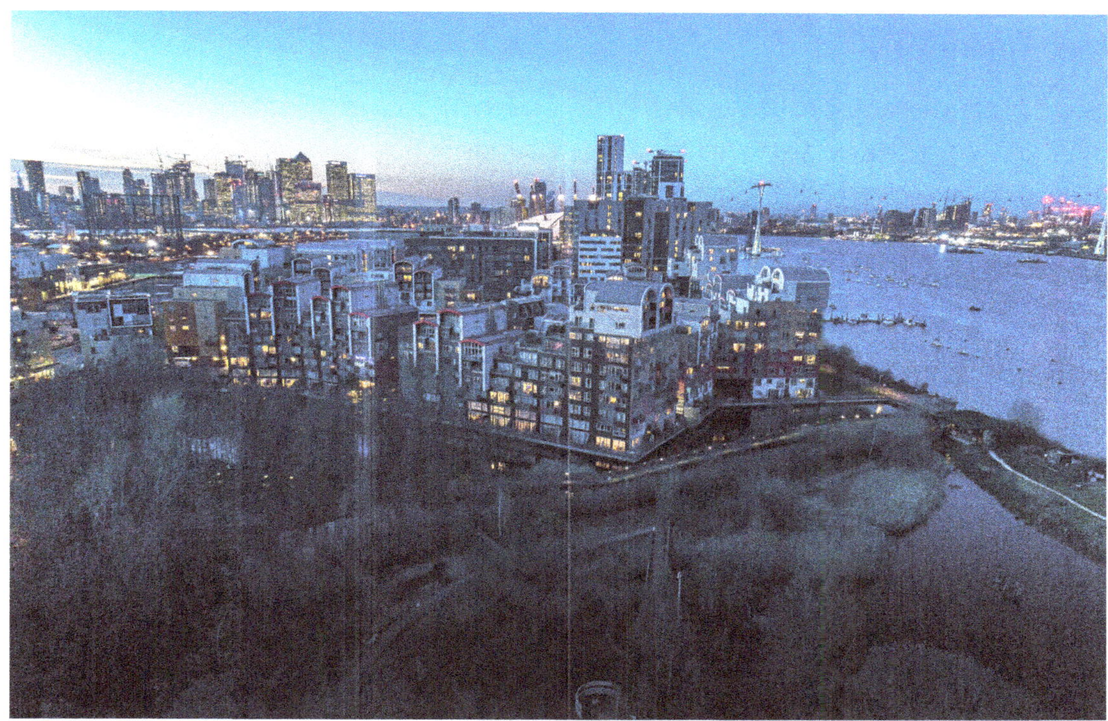

Characteristics of the Blue Hour:

1. Soft Blue Tones:

The sky transitions from vibrant sunset colours to deep blue, creating a calm and peaceful ambiance.

2. Contrast with Artificial Lights:

Cityscapes and landscapes come alive as artificial lights start to illuminate, creating a beautiful contrast with the natural blue tones.

3. Smooth Transitions:

The changing hues during the blue hour provide smooth transitions between light and dark, offering a cinematic quality to your drone photography.

4. Ideal for Cityscapes:

Urban environments are particularly captivating during the blue hour, as city lights and architecture stand out against the twilight sky.

Blue Hour Timing:

Summer: The blue hour follows the golden hour, lasting for approximately 30-40 minutes after sunset and before sunrise.

Winter: The blue hour is slightly shorter, typically around 20-30 minutes after sunset and before sunrise.

Shooting during the blue hour requires a good understanding of your drone's low-light capabilities. Consider using higher ISO settings and slower shutter speeds while ensuring image stabilization to combat the dwindling light.

Remember, the golden and blue hour is a fleeting spectacle. The actual duration varies with seasons and locations, so keep an eye on the clock. In winter, it might be more of a 'golden fifteen minutes,' but fear not, for those minutes are pure gold in the world of drone photography.

Mastering Long Exposure with Drones

Long exposure photography involves using extended shutter speeds to capture movement and create unique visual effects. Drones equipped with cameras open up exciting possibilities for long exposure shots from aerial perspectives.

The two keys are a slower shutter speed and increased ISO – experiment with settings to extend exposure time. It is better to increase the ISO rather than slow the shutter speed down too much because the drone does move around in the air. It is **not** like a tripod in the sky.

The key is to be flexible, work quickly and methodically. Start with the shutter speed and then move to the ISO. Take a selection of images at each setting before you move on to the next setting. Shutter speeds slower than 1/30 may cause blurring because the drone does move in the sky, depending on the wind speed.

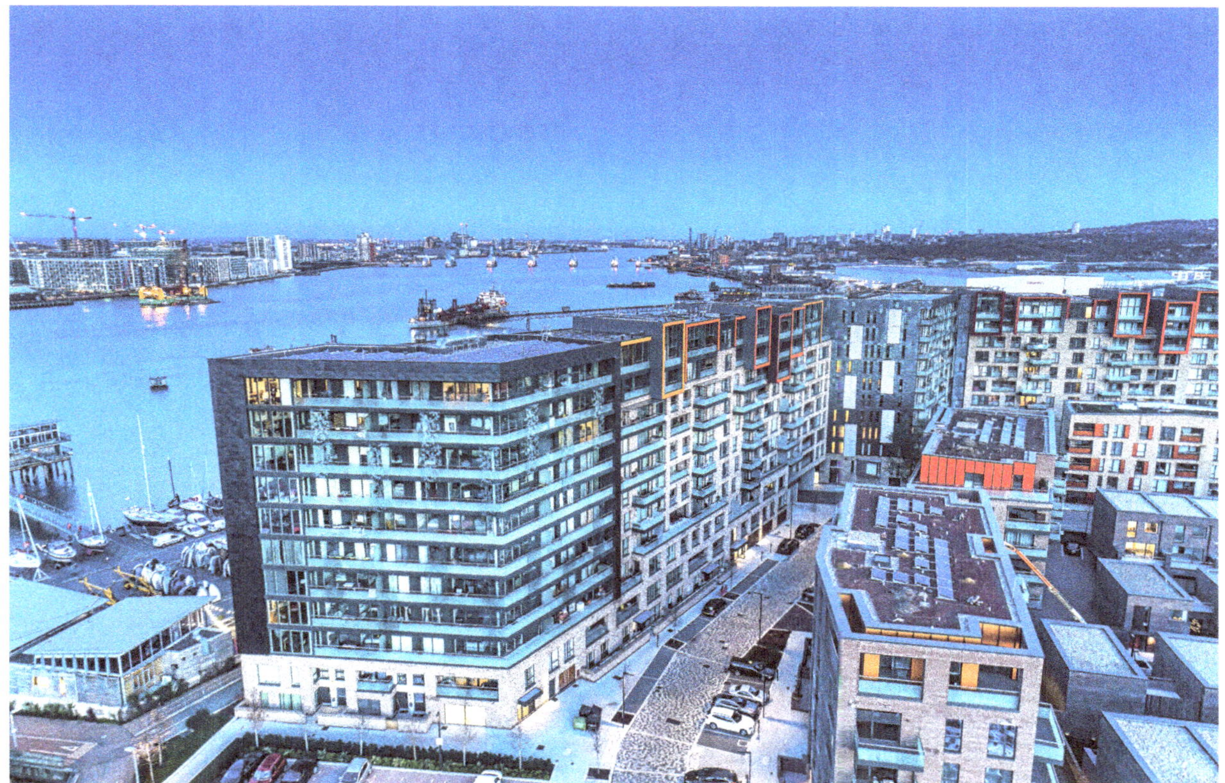

Tips for Long Exposure Drone Photography:

1. Stable Platform:

Ensure your drone is in a stable position before initiating a long exposure. This is crucial to avoid blurriness in the image. Shutter speeds slower that 1/30 will cause blurriness on a drone especially in windy conditions.

2. Use ND Filters:

Neutral Density (ND) filters reduce the amount of light entering the camera, allowing for longer shutter speeds. They are invaluable for achieving smooth, dreamy effects in long exposure shots.

3. Choose the Right Conditions:

Long exposure works best in low-light conditions or during the golden and blue hours when the light is subdued. This helps in avoiding overexposure due to extended shutter speeds.

4. Experiment with Movement:

Long exposure can capture the movement of clouds, water, or traffic trails. Experiment with different subjects to create dynamic and visually striking images.

5. Bracket Exposures:

If conditions are challenging, consider bracketing exposures and blending them in post-processing to achieve the desired effect without losing details.

ND Filters: Essential Tools for Long Exposure

Neutral Density (ND) filters are essential accessories for drone photographers engaging in long exposure photography. These filters limit the amount of light entering the camera, enabling the use of slower shutter speeds without overexposing the image.

It is not worth using any ND Filters on a drone at dusk as the light is going in the wrong direction. ND Filters only work with drones if light is strong or getting lighter (dawn).

Be aware that what you see as the image on the Drone Controller is not the same as the image on file. It may appear darker than the final file image. When you use an ND filter, you may have to wait until you review the still image files on your computer before you will see the final results of the image take with various ND filters.

You will not be able to use very slow shutter speed with a drone camera like you can with a camera on a tripod because the drone does move around. Really slow shutter speeds on a drone will result in blurred images.

Advantages of ND Filters:

1. Extended Shutter Speeds: ND filters allow for longer exposure times, crucial for achieving the desired effects in long exposure photography.

2. Control Over Exposure: ND filters provide precise control over exposure in varying lighting conditions, ensuring well-balanced and visually appealing shots.

3. Maintain Image Quality: By reducing the amount of light without affecting colour or sharpness, ND filters help maintain the overall image quality.

4. Creative Possibilities: ND filters open up creative possibilities, allowing drone photographers to experiment with different shutter speeds and capture movement in a way that conventional filters cannot.

5. Experimentation is Key: Explore the possibilities of creative expression by experimenting with different ND filter strengths.

Landscape Photography:

Practical Applications of Golden Hour, Blue Hour, and Long Exposure

Golden Hour: Capture landscapes bathed in warm, soft light, accentuating textures and creating stunning compositions.

Blue Hour: Cityscapes or landscapes illuminated by artificial lights against the twilight sky can result in captivating images.

Coastal and Water Photography:

Golden Hour: Enhance reflections on water surfaces and capture the glow of sunrise or sunset on coastal scenes.

Blue Hour: Capture the tranquillity of bodies of water with a serene blue background.

Urban Photography:

Golden Hour: Illuminate cityscapes with the warm glow of sunset, emphasizing architectural details.

Blue Hour: Create dramatic cityscapes with the interplay of artificial lights against the deep blue sky.

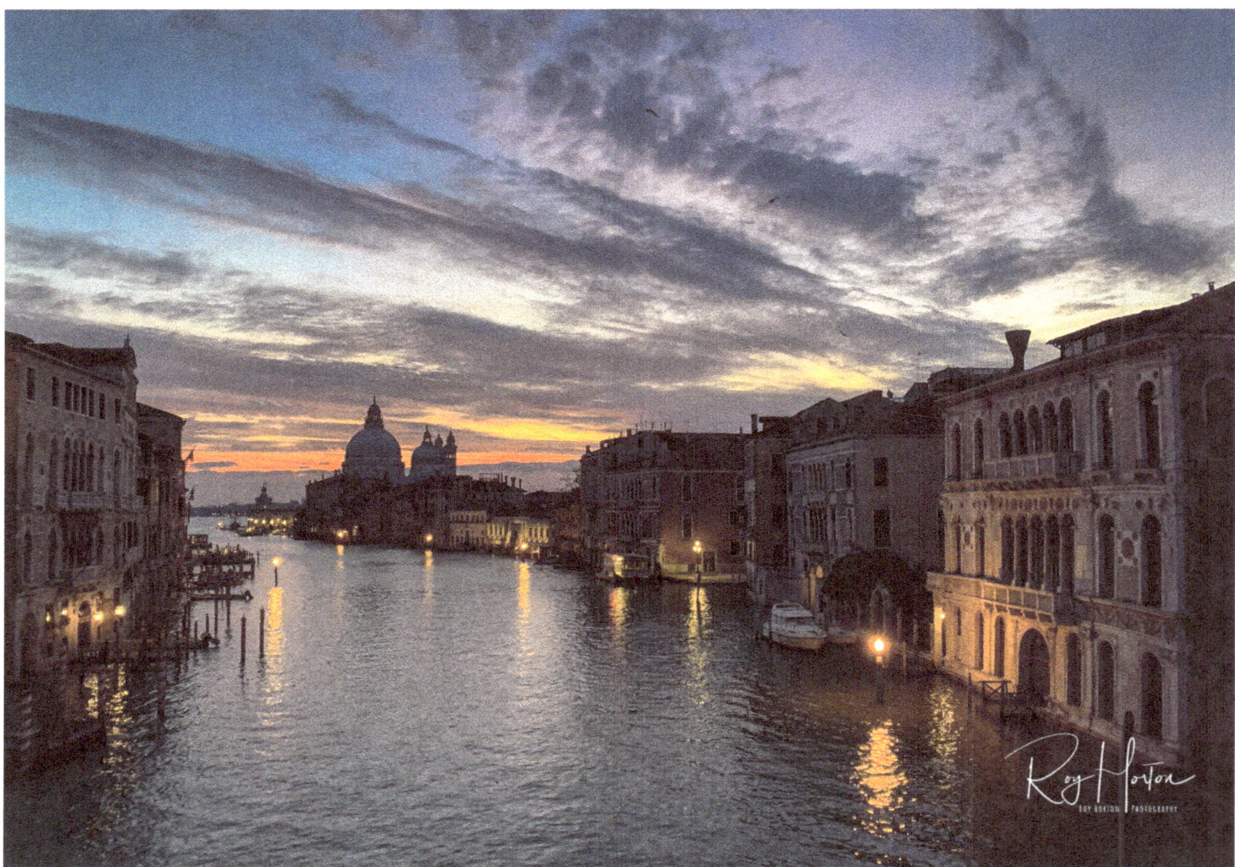

Long Exposure:

Light Trails: Capture mesmerizing light trails from moving vehicles, adding a dynamic and energetic element to urban scenes.

Cloud Movement: Experiment with extended exposures to capture the graceful movement of clouds, creating ethereal and dreamlike images.

Understanding the nuances of lighting conditions, especially during the golden hour, blue hour, and in long exposure scenarios, is akin to unlocking a treasure chest of creative possibilities. These magical hours offer unique atmospheres and aesthetics, setting the stage for captivating aerial imagery.

Framing and Perspective from the Sky

When flying a drone the viewpoint is different from a camera at ground level, because you are able to fly up to 400ft and change the gimbal angle. So each gimbal angle gives a different frame and perspective.

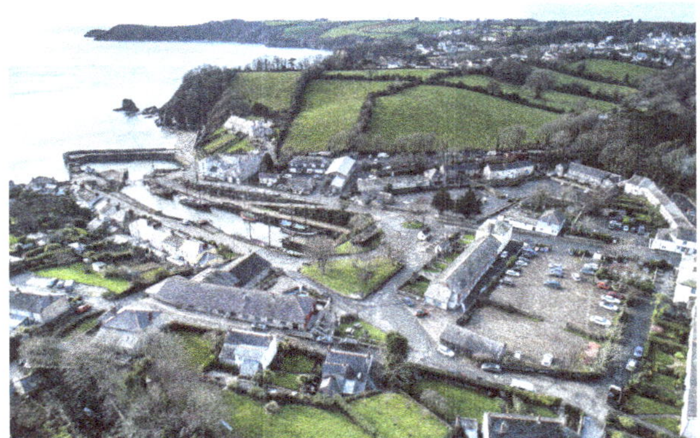
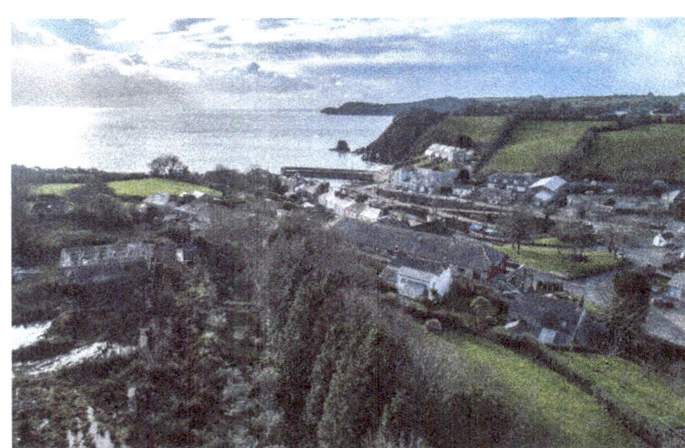

Depth and Distance: Explore the three-dimensional possibilities of aerial photography. From the heights of the sky, create compositions that convey depth, using elements in the foreground, midground, and background to tell your story.

Consider your frame as the stage for the viewer. Showcase techniques where framing directs attention, leading the eyes from one point to another, creating a narrative flow within your composition. Create focal points within the frame, drawing attention to key elements and telling stories from an aerial perspective.

Break down the misconception that aerial shots are just about capturing vast expanses. Use framing to turn a sprawling landscape into an intimate image.

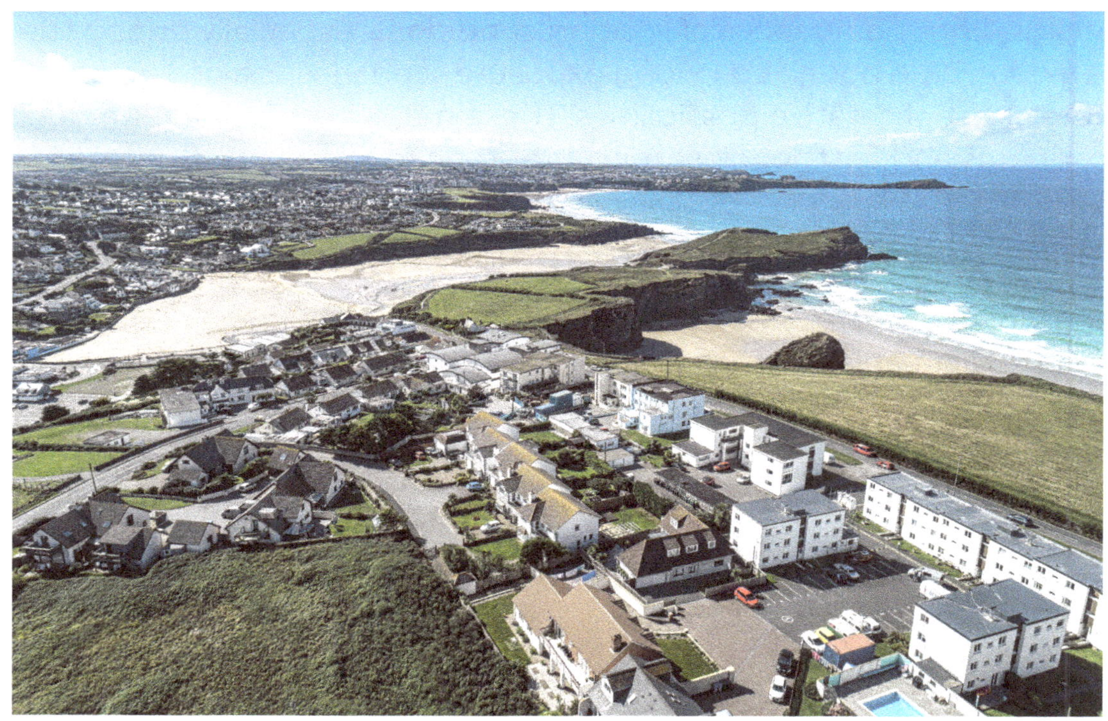

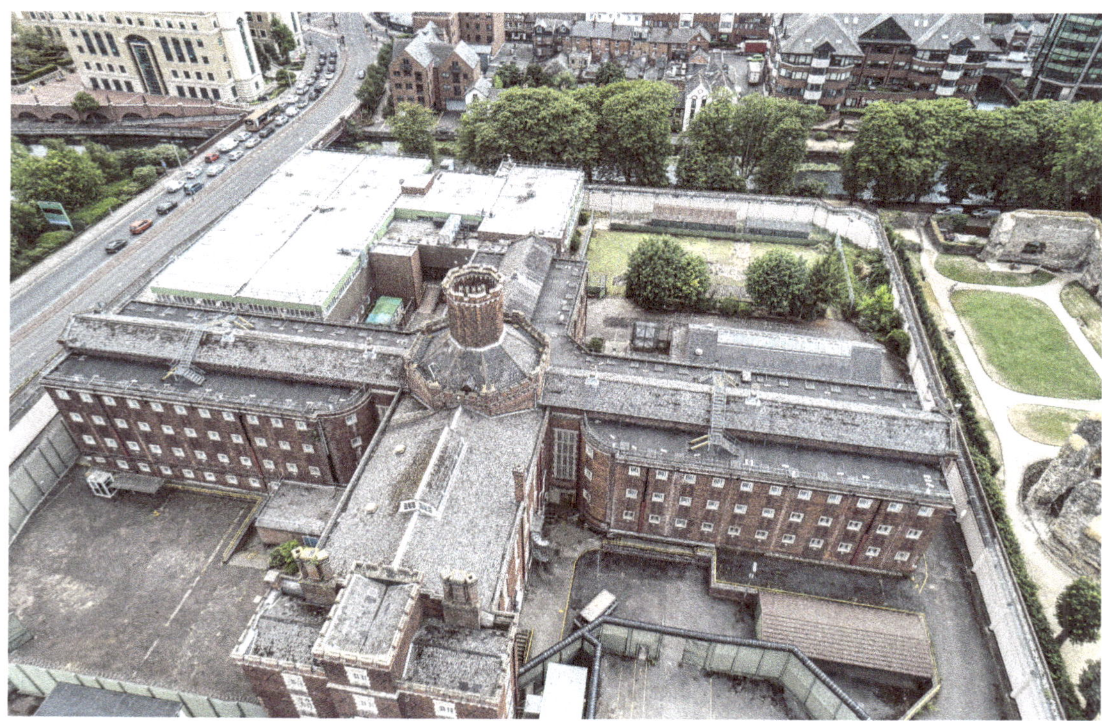

EDITING AND POST-PRODUCTION

Guide to Editing and Post-Production

There is a wide variety of editing software available free, on monthly subscription or outright purchase that runs on your computer, tablet or mobile phone.

Most editing software will improve your JPEG or RAW images. They will run on PC Windows and MAC Apple platforms.

Photo Editing Software gives you the power to adjust, transform, and enhance your images.

The software allows you to adjust exposure, balance light and shadows control brightness and contrast. Look for features to colour correct the images, by adjusting white balance, hues, and saturation control.

Learning about photo editing software allows you to achieve professional-level results, enhancing your photos for both personal satisfaction and potential commercial use. Photo editing software opens up a world of creative possibilities, allowing you to experiment with colours, textures, and effects to express your unique vision.

Enhancing and editing photos ensures that your memories are preserved in the best possible quality, creating lasting mementos for future generations. Learning widely-used software like Adobe Photoshop or Lightroom provides a versatile skillset that can be applied across computers, tablets, and mobile devices.

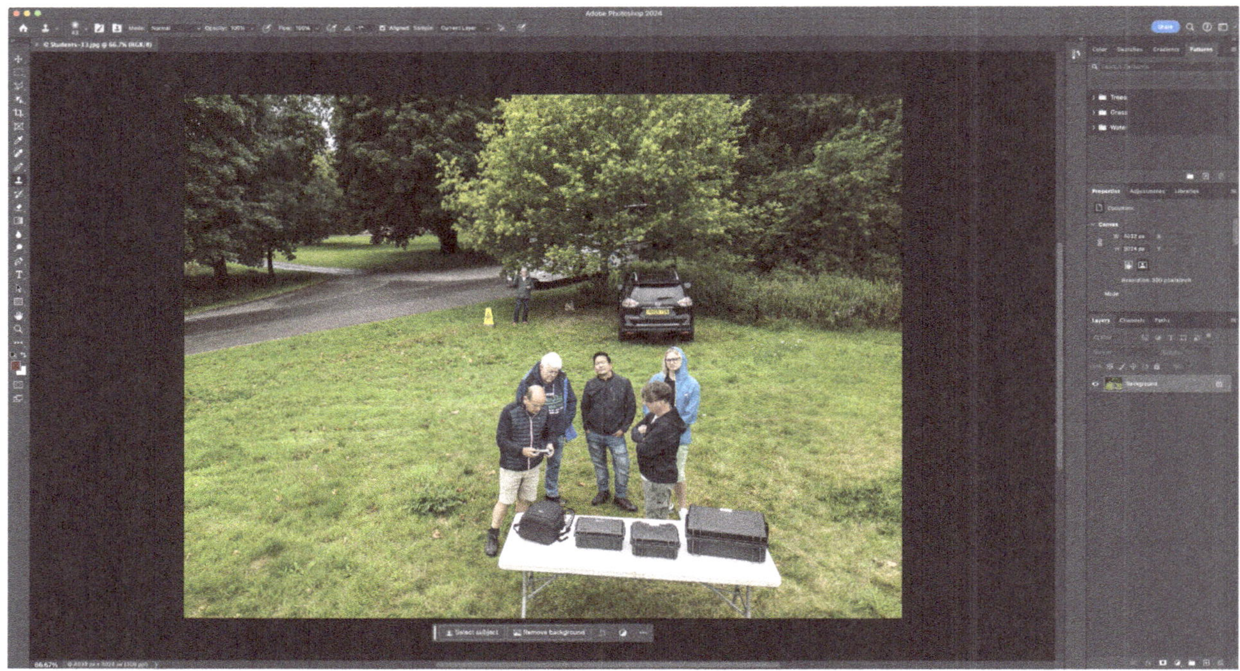

Top 10 Computer Photo Editing Software Packages

1. Adobe Photoshop:

Adobe Photoshop is a powerhouse in professional photo editing. It offers advanced features for image manipulation, retouching, and graphic design. With a vast array of tools and a supportive community, Photoshop is the industry standard.

2. Adobe Lightroom Classic:

Also from Adobe, Lightroom Classic is ideal for photo organization, RAW editing, and batch processing. Its non-destructive editing workflow makes it a favorite among photographers.

3. Capture One:

Capture One is known for its exceptional RAW processing capabilities. It offers powerful colour grading, tethered shooting support, and a customizable interface, making it a favorite among professional photographers.

4. DxO PhotoLab:

DxO PhotoLab excels in automatic corrections and intelligent image enhancement. Its advanced features include Prime Denoise technology and customizable workspaces.

5. Affinity Photo:

Affinity Photo is a cost-effective alternative to Photoshop. It boasts professional-grade features, including advanced layer editing, panorama stitching, and HDR support.

6. GIMP (GNU Image Manipulation Program):

GIMP is a free, open-source photo editing software that rivals commercial options. It provides a range of tools for image retouching, editing, and composition.

7. ON1 Photo RAW:

ON1 Photo RAW is an all-in-one photo editing solution. It combines photo organization, RAW editing, and effects in a seamless workflow.

8. Corel PaintShop Pro:

PaintShop Pro is a user-friendly option with a range of editing tools, filters, and creative effects. It's suitable for both beginners and intermediate users.

9. Luminar AI:

Luminar AI stands out with its use of artificial intelligence for automated enhancements. It's designed to simplify complex editing tasks, making it accessible for all skill levels.

10. Darktable:

Darktable is a free, open-source alternative for RAW processing. It features non-destructive editing and a variety of modules for fine-tuning images.

Top 10 Photo Editing Apps

1. Adobe Lightroom Mobile:

Lightroom Mobile (Right image) is a mobile extension of the desktop version, offering powerful editing tools, presets, and cloud synchronisation for a seamless workflow across devices.

2. Snapseed:

Snapseed, owned by Google, is a versatile mobile app with a wide range of editing tools. It's user-friendly yet robust, making it a popular choice for mobile photographers.

3. VSCO:

VSCO is known for its stylish filters and minimalistic interface. It's a creative tool for enhancing photos with a focus on simplicity and aesthetics.

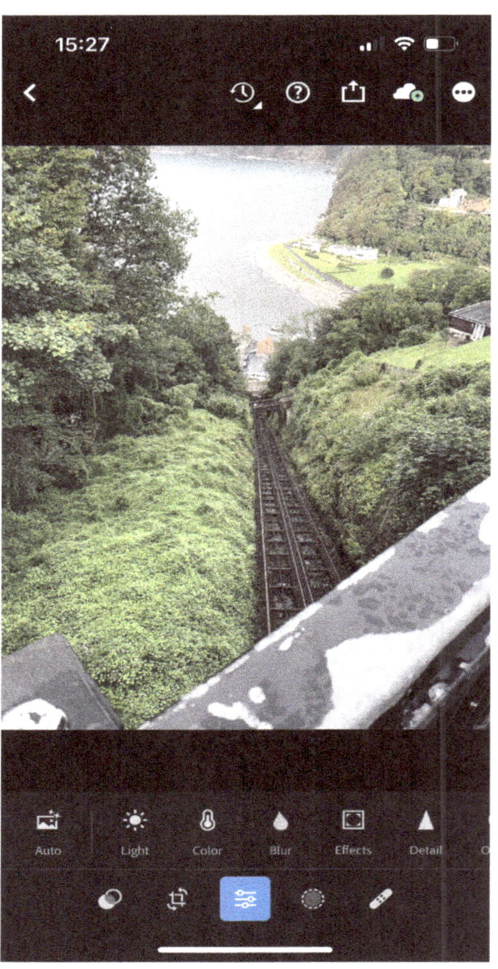

4. Afterlight:

Afterlight combines powerful editing tools with a user-friendly interface. It offers filters, textures, and frames to enhance your mobile photography.

5. Enlight:

Enlight is a comprehensive photo editing app that includes advanced features like selective adjustments, artistic filters, and creative blending modes.

6. Prisma:

Prisma uses artificial intelligence to transform photos into artworks inspired by famous artists. It offers a unique and artistic approach to photo editing.

7. TouchRetouch:

TouchRetouch specializes in removing unwanted elements from photos seamlessly. It's a handy tool for quick and easy retouching on the go.

8. Halide:

Halide is a powerful camera app with advanced manual controls. It's designed for photographers who want more control over their mobile photography.

9. Procreate Pocket:

Procreate Pocket is a pocket-sized version of the popular drawing app. It's ideal for those who want to unleash their creativity through digital art and photo editing on the go.

10. Adobe Photoshop Express:

Photoshop Express is a simplified version of its desktop counterpart. It offers essential editing tools for quick adjustments and enhancements on mobile devices.

Remember, the best software or app for you depends on your specific needs, preferences, and level of expertise. Whether you're a professional photographer or an amateur looking to enhance your Instagram photos, investing time in learning photo editing software can significantly elevate the quality of your visual creations.

PRINTING AND SHARING PHOTOS

In the digital age, where memories are captured with the click of a button, the desire to transform those digital images into tangible prints is stronger than ever. Whether you're looking to print a breathtaking aerial landscape, or a property, achieving the best possible results involves careful consideration of both the printing process and the choice of paper. In this guide, we'll explore the best ways to print images from a file, recommend the ideal paper for various purposes, and introduce the top 10 online printing services to bring your digital images to life.

Printing Process

1. Understand Colour Profiles

Before diving into the printing process, it's crucial to understand colour profiles. Colour profiles ensure consistency in colour representation across different devices. Common colour profiles include sRGB, Adobe RGB, and CMYK. Ensure your image is in the appropriate colour profile for your intended print output.

2. Image Resolution Matters

Resolution is key to achieving sharp and clear prints. For high-quality results, aim for an image resolution of at least 300 dots per inch (DPI). This ensures that the printed image maintains its clarity and detail, especially when enlarging.

3. Choose the Right File Format

JPEG is a widely used format for digital images, but it is a compressed format that may result in some loss of quality. For the best results, consider using uncompressed formats like TIFF or PNG when saving images for print.

4. Calibration and Colour Correction

Regularly calibrate your monitor to ensure accurate colour representation. Additionally, many online printing services offer colour correction options to fine-tune your images for optimal print quality.

Selecting the Right Paper

1. Photo Paper for Vibrant Colours

For printing photos with vibrant colours and sharp details, choose a high-quality photo paper. Glossy finishes enhance colour saturation, while matte finishes provide a more subdued, classic look.

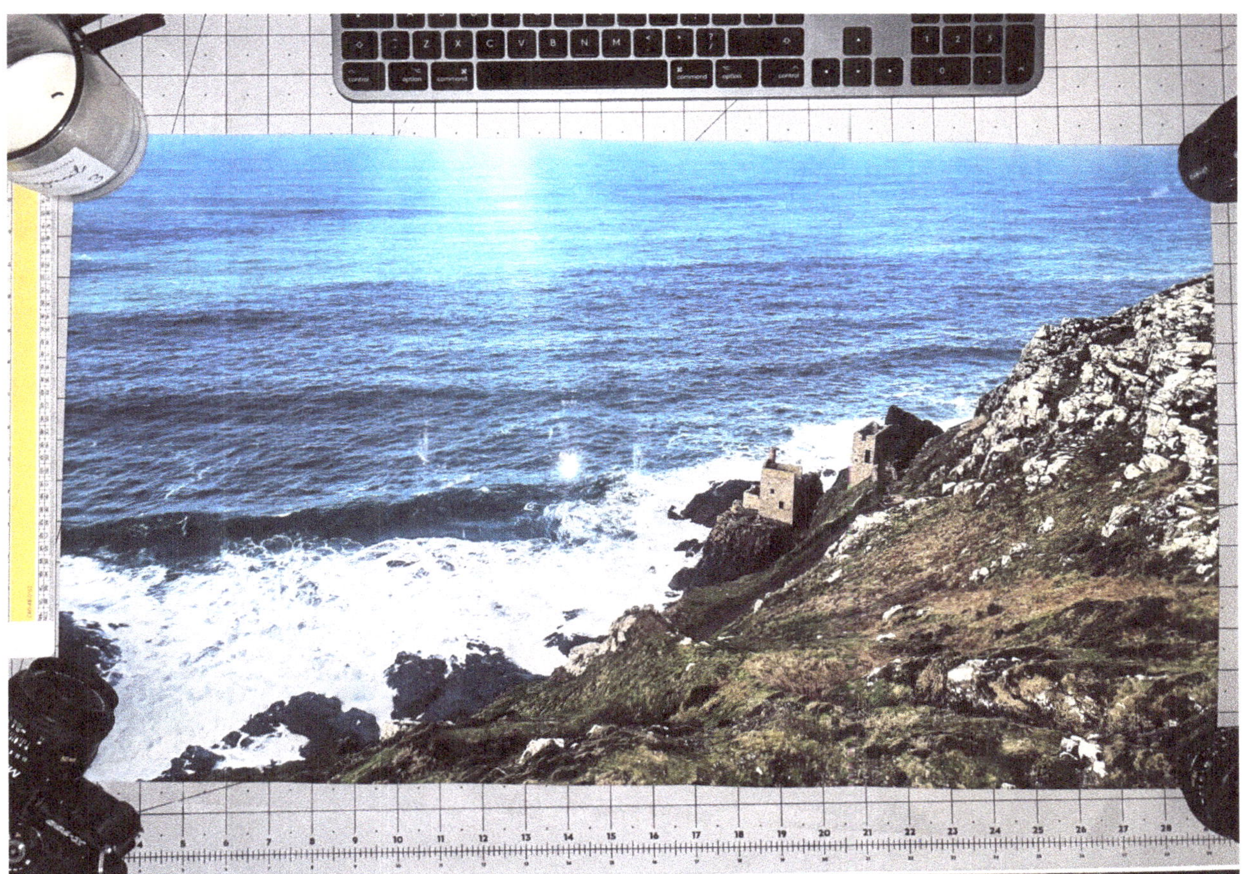

2. Fine Art Paper for Artistic Prints

If you're printing digital art or photographs with artistic intent, consider using fine art paper. This type of paper enhances the texture and feel of the print, providing a museum-quality appearance.

3. Canvas for a Timeless Look

Canvas prints add a timeless and artistic touch to your images. The texture of canvas gives a painting-like quality to your prints, making them suitable for both classic and contemporary settings.

4. Specialty Papers for Unique Finishes

Explore specialty papers for unique finishes. Metallic, pearl, and linen papers offer distinctive textures and appearances, allowing you to tailor your prints to match the mood and style of your images.

Top 10 Online Printing Services

Now that you've prepared your files and selected the ideal paper, it's time to explore the top 10 online printing services that consistently deliver high-quality prints.

1. Printique

Printique, formerly known as AdoramaPix, is renowned for its premium-quality prints and a wide range of customization options. From traditional prints to photo books and wall decor, Printique offers a variety of printing services to meet your needs.

2. Shutterfly

Shutterfly is a popular choice for its user-friendly interface and diverse product offerings. With a variety of paper options and the ability to create personalized photo books, cards, and gifts, Shutterfly provides a one-stop solution for all your printing needs.

3. Nations Photo Lab

Known for its professional-grade prints and quick turnaround times, Nations Photo Lab is a favourite among photographers. They offer a range of papers, including lustre, metallic, and deep matte, ensuring that your prints match your artistic vision.

4. Bay Photo Lab

Bay Photo Lab is a trusted name in the industry, offering a wide array of printing services. From metal prints to acrylic facemounts, Bay Photo Lab specializes in unique and high-quality printing options that cater to various preferences.

5. CanvasPop

If you're looking for top-notch canvas prints, CanvasPop is the go-to choice. With a focus on quality craftsmanship and attention to detail, CanvasPop turns your digital images into stunning canvas masterpieces.

6. MPIX

MPIX is known for its high-quality prints and excellent customer service. Whether you're printing standard photos or creating custom photo gifts, MPIX offers a range of products to suit your needs.

7. WhiteWall

WhiteWall is a premium online printing service that caters to those seeking museum-quality prints. With options like acrylic and aluminum prints, WhiteWall ensures that your images are presented in the most sophisticated and elegant manner.

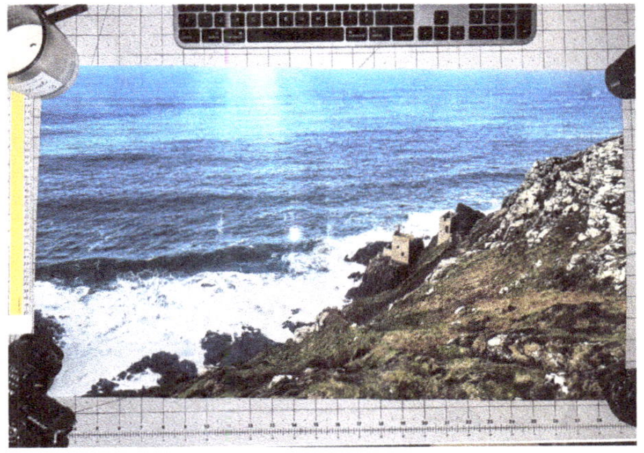

My 40 x 60cm bought from Whitewall

8. Printful

Printful is an excellent choice for those looking to sell their artwork or designs on various products. This print-on-demand service allows you to create and sell custom prints, apparel, and accessories without the need for inventory.

9. PrintNinja

PrintNinja specializes in high-quality printing for art books, comic books, and other publications. With a focus on offset printing, PrintNinja ensures exceptional colour accuracy and detail for large print runs.

10. Artifact Uprising

Artifact Uprising stands out for its commitment to sustainable and eco-friendly printing practices. They offer a range of products, including photo books, prints, and calendars, with a focus on high-quality materials and craftsmanship.

Printing digital images is a transformative process that allows you to bring your memories and creativity to life. By understanding the printing process, selecting the right paper, and choosing a reputable online printing service, you can ensure that your prints not only meet but exceed your expectations. Whether you're creating a gallery wall of family photos or selling your artwork, the combination of thoughtful preparation and the right printing partner will result in stunning, long-lasting prints that you can cherish for years to come.

Selling Images Online

Selling your images online has become a popular way for photographers and artists to monetise their work. Here are ten of the best platforms where you can upload and sell your images, along with details on their commission structures:

1. Adobe Stock

Adobe Stock offers contributors a commission rate between 20% and 60%, depending on the contributor's level and whether the image is exclusive to Adobe Stock.

2. Shutterstock

Shutterstock operates on a tiered system. Contributors start at a 15% commission, which can increase to 40% as their lifetime earnings with Shutterstock increase.

3. Getty Images / iStock

Getty Images and iStock have different commission structures. Getty Images generally offers higher commissions but is more selective. iStock pays contributors based on a percentage, with rates varying between 15% and 45%.

4. Alamy

Alamy offers a straightforward commission rate of 50% for each sale, making it one of the more generous options in the stock photography market.

5. Pond5

Pond5 allows contributors to set their own prices, and they receive 50% of each sale. This platform is known for its flexibility and diverse content offerings beyond just photos.

6. Etsy

Etsy charges a 5% transaction fee and a 3% + $0.25 payment processing fee for each sale. While Etsy is not exclusively a stock photo platform, it provides a marketplace for artists and photographers to sell their work.

7. SmugMug

SmugMug operates on a subscription-based model for photographers. You can set your own pricing, and SmugMug takes a percentage ranging from 15% to 85%, depending on your subscription level.

8. **500px**

500px has a custom licensing system where contributors can set their own prices for licensing images. The platform takes a 30% commission on licensing sales.

9. **EyeEm**

EyeEm offers a 50% commission on each sale. The platform also allows contributors to distribute their images to other stock photo websites.

10. **Foap**

Foap provides a 50% commission for each photo sold. Foap is known for its mobile-first approach, allowing users to upload and sell photos directly from their smartphones.

It's essential to carefully read the terms and conditions of each platform, as commission structures and licensing agreements may change. Additionally, consider the specific audience and niche of each platform to determine which aligns best with your target market.

Keep in mind that exclusivity agreements and licensing terms can impact your earnings, so choose the platform that best suits your needs and goals as a photographer or artist.

TROUBLESHOOTING COMMON ISSUES

Here are some of the common issues we have seen in the last six years of flying and training new students.

Blurred Photos

1. Gimbal Shakes and vibrations – it is much better to take a still image when the drone is stationary in the sky, rather than flying at speed. It allows you to frame the shot before you shoot and there is less chance of the drone moving around as the shutter takes the photo.

2. Subject in Motion: - If your subject is moving a faster shutter speed is recommended to stop the subject turning into a fuzzy blur. You can use tracking shots which will follow your subject's next move.

3. Forgetting to Focus - Focus is the heartbeat of a sharp image. If you use auto-focus, always remember to click on you focus point with the green box on your controller screen before every image you take. Use the same approach for every manual focus click on your white box focus point before taking every image.

Overexposure/Underexposure: Balancing the Light

In the drone app there are two feature you can enable to help show you parts of the image that are over or under exposed.

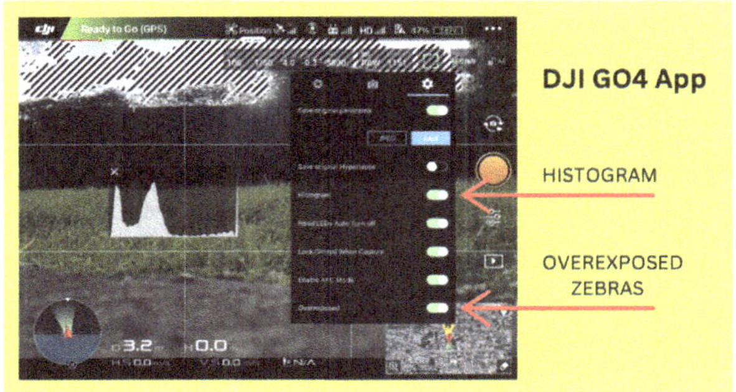

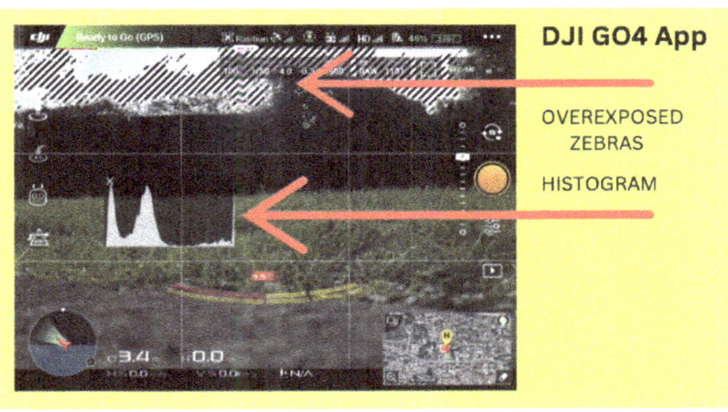

These features are the helpful histogram and the black and white zebra over exposure warning.

You can also see overexposed and underexposed image on the controller screen, but the screen may not show you what you are taking because it is in a lower resolution. If you have an ND Filter on the lens, it will also look darker, so the Histogram is the best tool to trust.

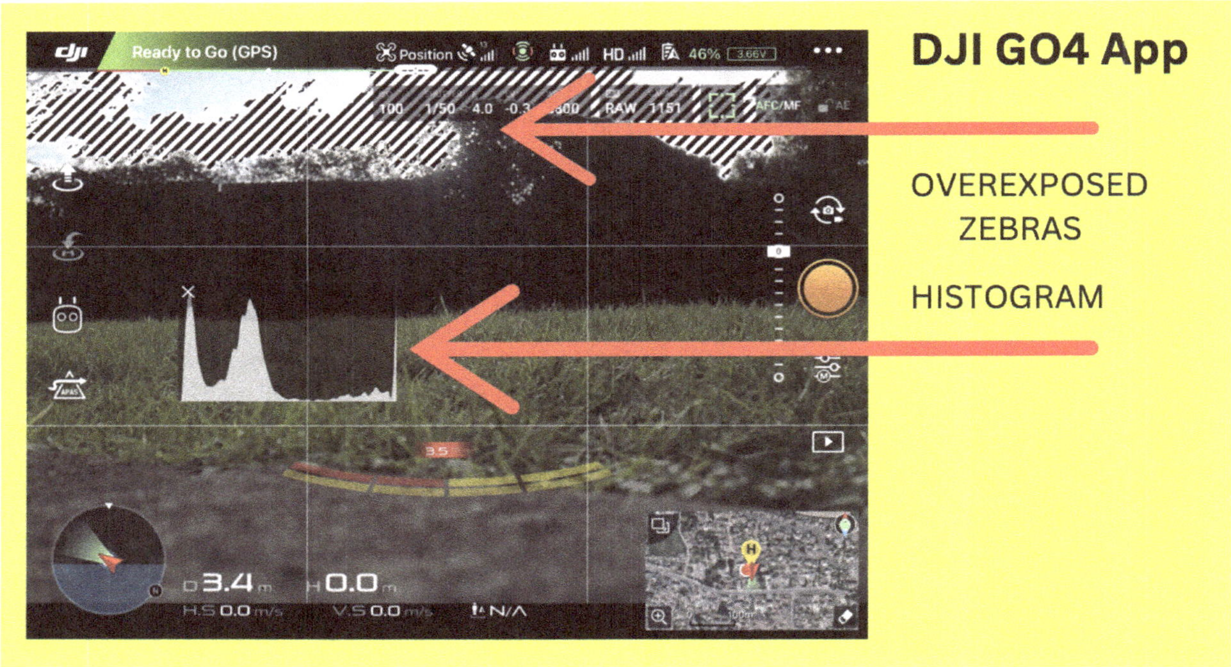

On the app for most DJI Drones there is a exposure circle to click on which changes the exposure to the point in the exposure circle.

Compositional Woes

1. Your image is Cluttered: learn the art of simplicity, (less is more) discover the rule of thirds and remove any visual chaos from your aerial landscapes.

2. Awkward Angles and Distracting Elements: Remove any distracting elements, fly the drone backwards, forwards, left, right and up or down to find the best angel and shot. Use this to control your visual narrative. Don't expect to put the drone in the air and get the perfect shot first time, you may need to fly to many positions and height before you see the right shot.

3. Visual Harmony and Balance: This comes from simplifying your images and experience. It is personal choice we all see things in different ways. But you need leading lines that guide the viewer's gaze to framing that elevates your subjects and atmosphere. If the image is boring when it's taken, it will be boring when you edit it.

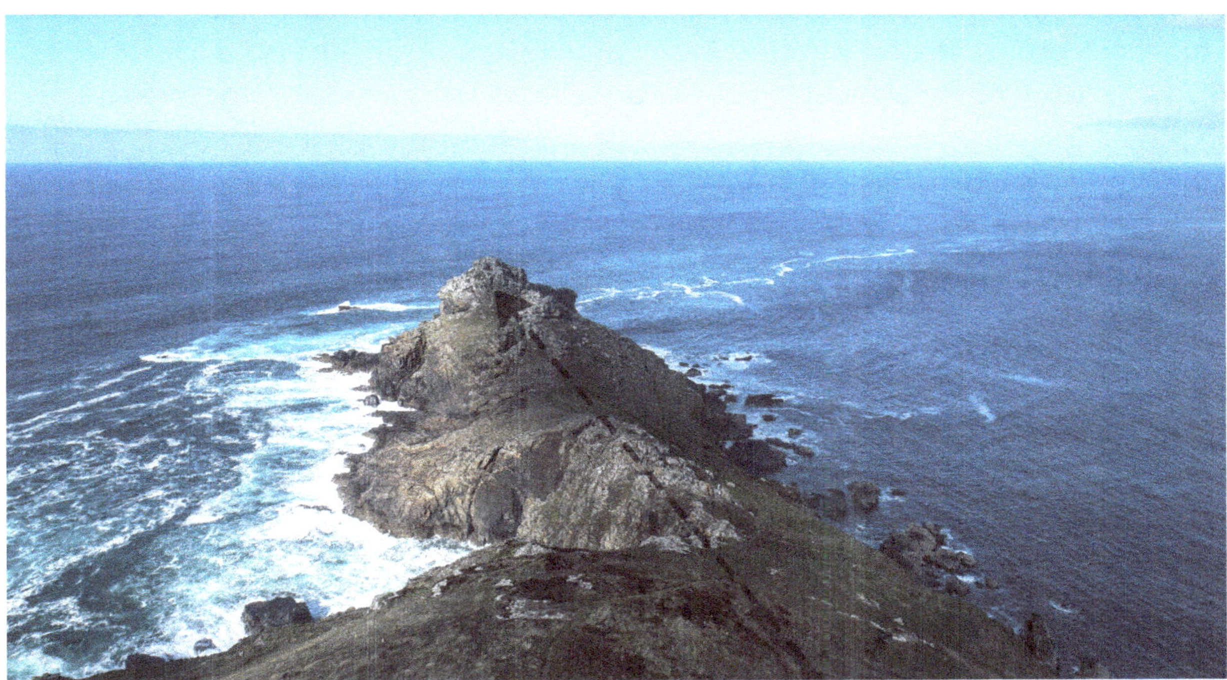

CONCLUSION

Final Advice for Better Drone Photography

Eternal Students of the Sky: - The pursuit of drone photography is a lifelong class. Never let the excitement of learning escape your wingspan. Each new skill, each fresh insight, adds a feather to your cap of mastery.

Wings of Practice: - The sky is vast, and so are your possibilities. Practice is your secret weapon. Regularly spread your photographic wings, and with each flight, you'll gain altitude in skill and confidence.

Risk, Experiment, Capture: - In the sky of creativity, turbulence often leads to the most breathtaking images. Don't shy away from risks and experiments. Some of the most captivating shots arise from the clouds of uncertainty.

Critique with Compassion: - Evaluate your images with a kind and objective eye. Celebrate what works, learn from what doesn't, and let the process of critique be a gentle breeze that propels you forward.

Community Connection: - Join the flock! Connect with fellow drone photographers in communities and clubs. The camaraderie of like-minded artists is a tailwind that propels everyone further.

Wings Ready, Camera Steady: - Keep your drone companion by your side. The best photo opportunities often soar in unannounced. Be ready to capture the magic, whether it's a breathtaking landscape or an unexpected moment.

Trust Your Inner Pilot: - While technical knowledge is your co-pilot, trust your artistic instincts as the captain of your photographic journey. Your intuition is the wind beneath your creative wings.

Pre-Flight Set Up - Check List

Based on the things you have learned in this guide here is a short setup check list of the settings you should consider before you fly your drone.

Focus: Choose auto or manual focus. Remember to press the focus point on the screen with your finger before you take each photo.

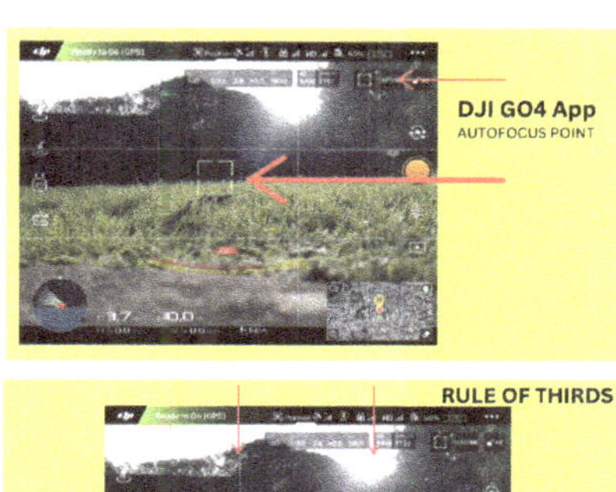

Composition: Switch on Rule of Thirds lines in the DJI App. Move your focus object to one of the four cross points.

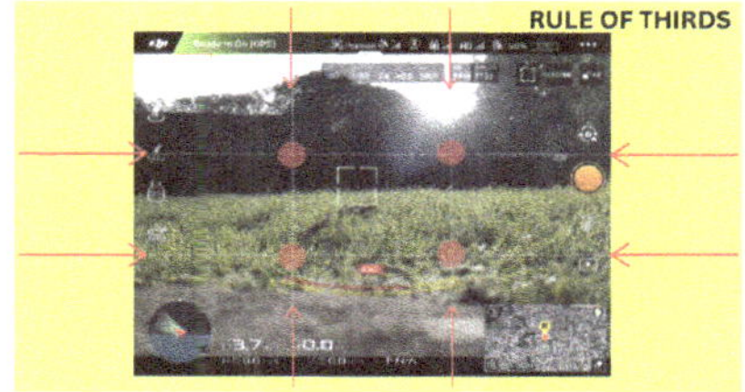

Shutter Speed: Set your shutter speed on manual or priority at the sweet spot for your drone - 1/50 sec. If you use auto make sure shutter speed doesn't not go below 1/30.

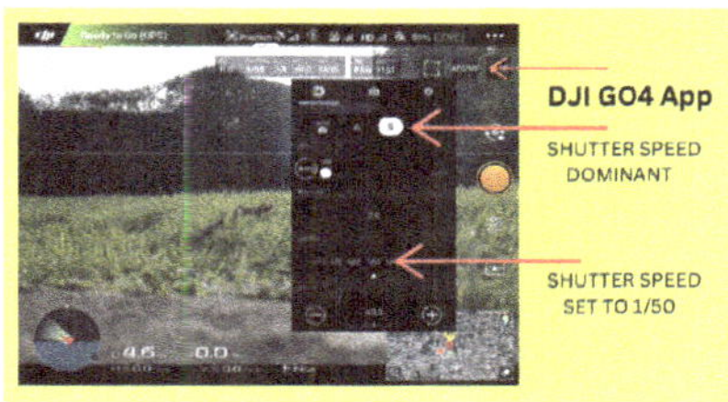

Aperture: Set your aperture on manual or priority at the sweet spot for your drone - f4.0 or f5.6. If your DJI drone has a fixed aperture adjust Shutter speed and ISO.

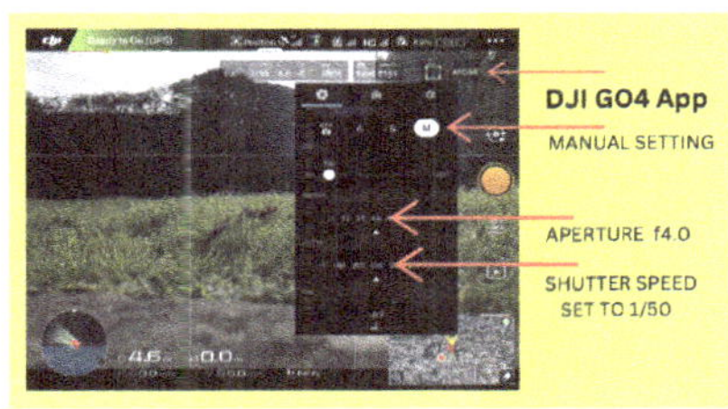

ISO: Set your ISO to 100 or 200 for normal light conditions. Increase ISO up to 1600 for low light or use the low light setting in the App.

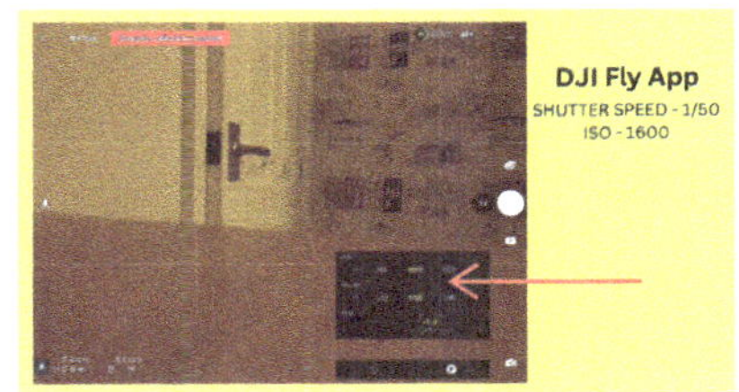

Dynamic Range: Look at light conditions. Use AEB or HDR modes if the light is affecting the highlights or shadows.

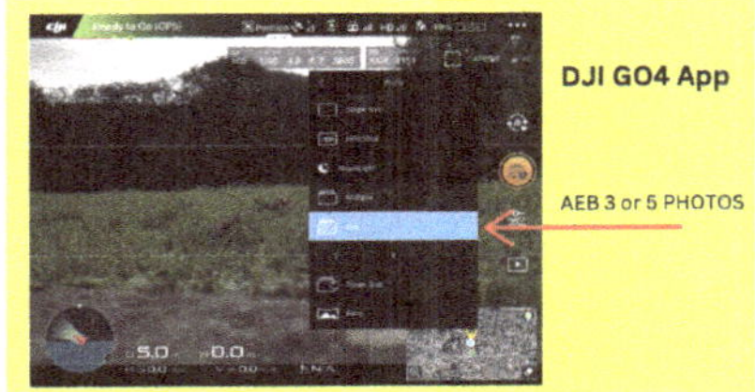

White Balance: Set white balance between 5,300-6,400k depending on the light conditions. 5,800k is typical for normal daylight.

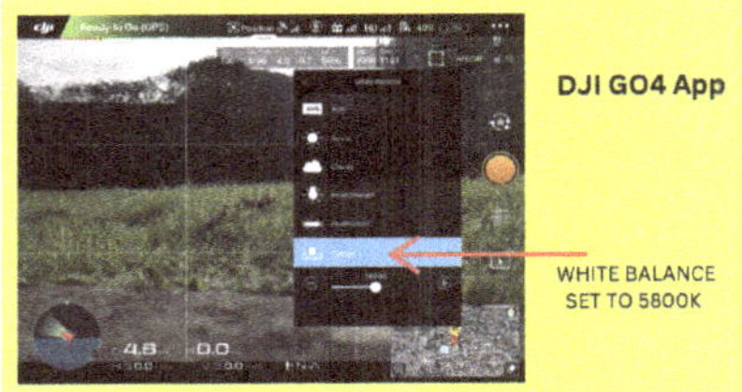

Sharpness: Set the sharpness to -2 in the triangle settings in the DJI App.

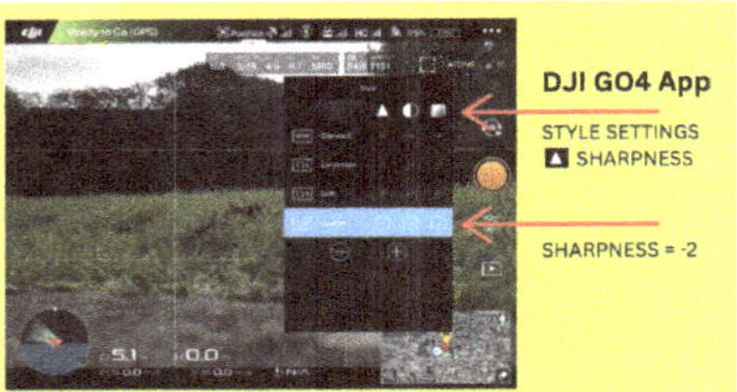

Image Format: Select your image format. JPEG, RAW or JPEG and RAW.

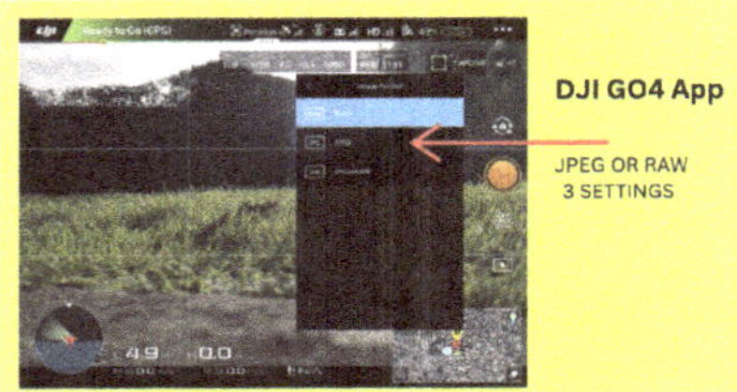

Over Exposure/Under Exposure: Switch on the Histogram, The histogram indicator should be showing predominantly in the middle of the range.

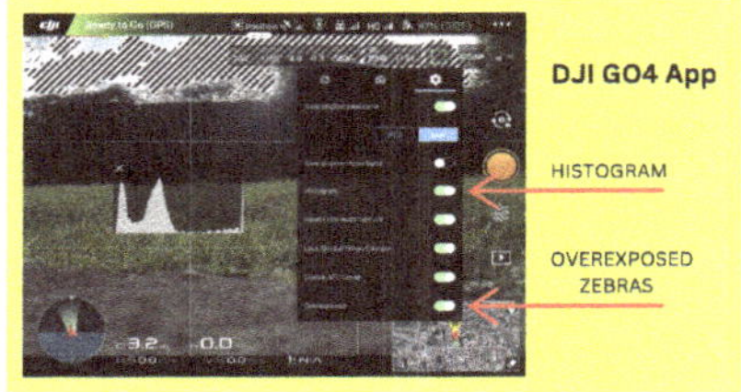

ND Filters: Choose your ND Filter for the light conditions. ND 8 for a cloudy day going up to ND32 for a very sunny day

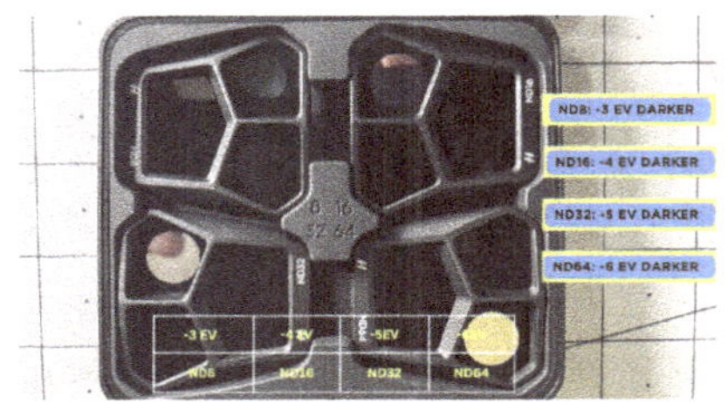

ISBN: 978-1-0686498-0-6

Publisher: Roy Horton and Drone School UK

Published in 2024

Email: roy@droneschooluk.co.uk